TITI
ALL THE BEST TO YOU
& GOOD LUCK!

WOLF

© Copyright 2007 Wolf Wilbert.
All rights reserved. No part of this publication may be reproduced, stored in a retrieval system, or transmitted, in any form or by any means, electronic, mechanical, photocopying, recording, or otherwise, without the written prior permission of the author.

Note for Librarians: A cataloguing record for this book is available from Library and Archives Canada at www.collectionscanada.ca/amicus/index-e.html
ISBN 1-4251-1331-1

Printed in Victoria, BC, Canada. Printed on paper with minimum 30% recycled fibre.
Trafford's print shop runs on "green energy" from solar, wind and other environmentally-friendly power sources.

Offices in Canada, USA, Ireland and UK

Book sales for North America and international:
Trafford Publishing, 6E–2333 Government St.,
Victoria, BC V8T 4P4 CANADA
phone 250 383 6864 (toll-free 1 888 232 4444)
fax 250 383 6804; email to orders@trafford.com

Book sales in Europe:
Trafford Publishing (UK) Limited, 9 Park End Street, 2nd Floor
Oxford, UK OX1 1HH UNITED KINGDOM
phone +44 (0)1865 722 113 (local rate 0845 230 9601)
facsimile +44 (0)1865 722 868; info.uk@trafford.com

Order online at:
trafford.com/06-3090

10 9 8 7 6 5 4 3 2

INDEX

FOREWORD	By Klaus D. Hoffman	
CREDITS	Thank You	1
INTRODUCTION	Thoughts about the Building Industry	2
IN THE BEGINNING	How it all Started	4
SYSTEM CONNECTIONS	Typical Post & Beam Connections	9
WHAT IS THE HOOK&BUILD™ BUILDING SYSTEM?	Explaining the System	14
THE DESIGN	How to Start Out with a Good Design	19
STEP BY STEP	Getting the System Installed Correctly	25
FOUNDATION SYSTEMS	Which Foundation to Choose	32
FLOOR SYSTEMS	Different Floor Solutions	34
WALL SYSTEMS	Knowing the Walls	36
ROOF SYSTEMS	Roof Ideas	40
FINISHES	Without Limitations	42

INDEX

BUILDING DETAILS

EMERGENCY CONCEPTS

RESOURCES

ABOUT THE AUTHOR

Endless Possibilities   44

Helping the Ones in Need   73

Handy Addresses   77

    79

FOREWORD

Horse drawn carriages are no longer the means of transportation. Typewriters have disappeared and been replaced by computers and associated advanced technologies.

It is interesting to note that in one area of architecture and design the natural evolutionary process has been moving only very slowly. Most of our housing and smaller building designs still reflect the manual typewriter era - the stick built, cut and nail, construction approach.

It takes an open mind to see the shortcomings of the past, understand the needs for the future and then with focus and determination, create the solutions. Mr. Wolf Wilbert has these capacities. He, after many years of consciously focused development, created the Hook&Build™ Building System, a wonderful technology which harmoniously brings together a whole range of design and construction related benefits in this area of architecture.

The technology can now be accessed by architects and developers for use everywhere and the outdated "stick built" approach can begin its transformation.

I am very grateful to have met Mr. Wolf Wilbert already in the seventies when he was working as a design architect for the City of Edmonton. During the development of his system, his view has always been global, from simple shelter units for Third World countries to any other kind of housing as well as commercial developments, anywhere.

The time, cost, quality, longevity and flexibility benefits of the Hook&Build™ Building System as its earthquake resistance, are phenomenal.

When mind and heart work together, many partnerships will be develop and the fruits of the purpose of Mr. Wilbert's professional life can benefit all of humanity.

Klaus D. Hoffman

GIVING CREDIT

THANK YOU!

It took me many years to come to the point of writing this book. Along the way there were many ups and downs, happy moments, disappointments and frustrations. In all of these situations there were people involved - family and friends who supported my idea and believed in me and in my invention of the Hook&Build™ Building System.

Now it is time for me to say how much I appreciate all of you. There are too many to name and I wouldn't want to leave any of you out. When you receive a copy of this book with a hand written note from me in it, then you will know you figured in my efforts in a big way.

For now, I just want to thank you all from deep within my heart. You gave me hope and faith to see the bigger picture. God bless you all!

The Thought is the Creation of Reality

INTRODUCTION

Comments in this introduction are copied from the Hook&Build™ website: http://web.mac.com/wwilbert1

When will we learn?
Pictures of devastation and incredible loss..... We find them everywhere. Not only are poor countries hit by these natural disasters, such as the recent earthquake in Pakistan where thousands of people were left homeless or are missing, but North America experiences tornadoes and hurricanes as well, causing extensive damage and leaving thousands homeless as in the New Orleans disaster of 2005.

Did we learn from it? Did we rethink the way we build our homes, and try to rebuild with better solutions? Some do, but most of us rebuild the same way as before. Why? Most of us don't know any better, because there is no other alternative .... or is there?

For over fifteen years Wolf Wilbert has been researching, developing and inventing a new building technology. The Hook&Build™ Building System has its roots in Alberta, and has the potential to be an Alberta invention and building technology used by every country on this planet. This new technology arrives at a time in North America where the shortage of skilled trades people is more serious every year.

The masters in these trades are between 45 to 65 years old, and they are retiring fast. The younger generation is not interested in entering an aging technology, where 2x4s are still cut on site, then nailed together stick by stick, under any weather condition, the same way it was 50 years ago.

With his new Hook&Build™ Building System, Wolf has maintained the flexibility of the stick-built construction method, at the same time he has improved quality and building standards, by prefabricating the components of the structures in factories, and assembling them in record time on site.

The result is a far stronger building system than the stick-built technology. Even more important, this new technology will not harm the traditional finishing techniques used in the wood-frame building industry. A new kind of trade will be created for installers, erectors and others, opening new working opportunities for our youth around the world.

The many benefits of the Hook&Build™ Building System include:

- **high energy efficiency**
- **significant time savings**
- **much less waste**
- **30 per cent less wood material**
- **higher quality**
- **building designed to last for generations**
- **earthquake resistant structures**

INTRODUCTION

Wolf Wilbert is determined to teach this new technology to anyone willing to open his/her mind and listen. His greatest enthusiasm is directed to young people including engineering and architectural students, yet professionals, contractors, and people of any trade are welcome and encouraged to work with him. There will be seminars and workshops, and on-site hands-on learning experiences available for all who have a genuine interest in learning about this new approach to building.

In Wolf's opinion, stick - built construction has become an obsession in North America, with people hesitant to ask questions or make changes. It is important to evaluate carefully the pros and cons in this industry, and to adapt to the coming changes in the world.

Wolf is concerned that economic and environmental changes soon will force us to rethink our position. Therefore we should seek more realistic solutions to how we construct buildings. Traditional construction methods have failed, especially in areas hit by hurricanes, tsunamis, earthquakes and other natural disasters. The Hook&Build™ Building System offers a viable, cost effective, accessible solution for all.

When Wolf built the first project with the Hook&Build™ Building System for an engineer in Calgary, he instructed the contractor hired for the project to wait for Wolf's arrival on the site. The complete framing package was already delivered, and the crew awaited Wolf's instructions.

To their astonishment, Wolf asked them to move their compressors for the power tools, their tool belts, and especially their hammers aside. **"There will be no measuring, cutting or nailing on this frame. Everything is already done in the factory; all you need is this ratchet wrench to build the frame structure."** They looked at him in disbelief, but after the first components were erected, they started to have fun with the system. Four days later the frame was totally completed on this 3,000 square-foot home.

At another project near Red Deer, a reporter from the Edmonton Journal was on site. She asked one of the crew members what they thought about this new building system that they had not seen before. The answer was: **"It's like working with *Lego*; it is just bigger."** This 15,000 square-foot frame structure was erected in 7.5 days.

IN THE BEGINNING
HOW EVERYTHING STARTED

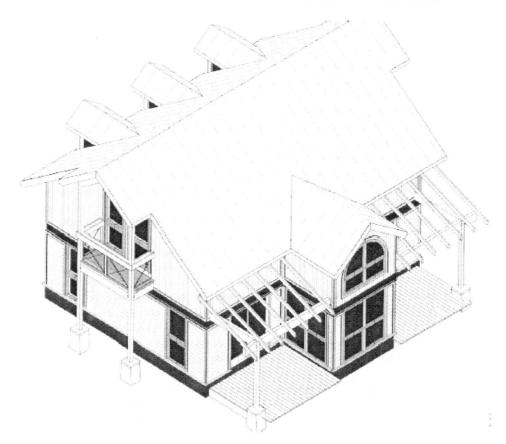

SAMPLE HOME

IN THE BEGINNING

HOW IT ALL STARTED

As I write this book, I mark my 25th anniversary as an independent architectural design consultant in Canada. I thought this is an opportune time to pursue my long-held aim to write a book about the Hook&Build™ Building System. For years I had intended to do so; however my busy schedule always seemed to get in the way. Finally in 2005 I decided to change courses and devote my time to promoting the Hook&Build™ Building System. This book is a part of my campain to tell the building industry and the home buyers about the merits of this superior system.

For many years I was a design consultant for architectural firms on large projects including schools, hospitals, churches, office buildings, court houses. Some of these projects were my own, and I carried them out from the design phase to the completion stage.

In the early eighties, when the economy nose dived, I was fortunate enough to be awarded with some projects in Inuvik, NWT.
I enjoyed the challenge of designing for permafrost conditions, and the experience gave me new knowledge in a very specific construction technology.

I learned very quickly the importance of finishing the working drawings as fully as possible - to make sure every detail is included and specified in the documents. The office structure I built was completed on time, on budget - without a single change order.

In the North, everything has to be shipped or flown in, or one has to wait until winter, when transport trucks are able to cross the ice.

To this end, I realized how much improvisation comes into play, especially in housing construction. I thought there must be a better way to build, but everybody was tuned into the stick build construction, as if there was nothing else available.

Next best are mobile homes or modular housing. However, the shipping costs are high, and the structures themselves were not really built for this kind of transportation. The long trip does not help these units, and so the result is not much better then buildings built from scratch on site.

The only solution I thought would be to build these homes the way IKEA™ builds furniture- have all the parts prefabricated as a package, and assemble it quickly on site. (Time is the essence in the north).

On searching all existing technologies, the post and beam structure stood out. It made perfect sense to me to develop this building technology further, as this type of structure has lasted for hundred of years all over the world and has proven its strength and beauty in many ways, as seen in timber frame homes of North America.

What inhibited my idea to build homes like IKEA™, was the right device or hardware to lock all pieces together with great strength. First I looked through all my catalogues to find a fitting device that would do the task simply, effectively and economically. No such luck! Searching the Internet proved fruitless. So I started to work on the problem myself

IN THE BEGINNING

for many weeks and months, whenever I had time to spare, until frustration overwhelmed me. Whatever I came up with would do only certain aspects of the task, or would not be strong enough, or just far too expensive to produce, or too complicated to install.

But I was so fascinated with the idea, I could not give up, and so I kept on trying. One sunny morning, sitting at my desk in my office, fumbling around with all kind of sketches, another idea came to me. At first I thought it never would work; it is just too simple. The more I worked on my sketch the more I realized I was on the right track. Shortly after that, the "Hook&Build™" device was born. This device is the most versatile locking hardware in the construction industry. It is multi-functional for all kinds of applications, making it a powerful tool to build shapes and forms where other hardware would simply not work anymore, or would be far too complicated and expensive to produce.

The next step was to go to the patent lawyer's office. Anyone who has gone through this process knows how secretive one has to be with a new invention, before one can go out and talk about it, or even to prepare prototypes for testing. Now this is all history, many buildings are built with the system I devised.

Last year the geodesic dome of a close friend burned down. I asked her what she would build now. She wanted another dome house. I did not try to change her mind and left it at that. One day her son came to town visiting several home suppliers, and also to chat with me about certain products and details. At one point he looked at my Hook&Build™ Building System™ display, and said that it is too bad I was not able to use the system to built a dome structure. I answered that I could build almost anything with the system, including a dome structure. He looked baffled at me and asked: "How would you do that?"

Using my Wonder board, I made a sketch and showed him how I would design the arches for the dome structure. He was impressed and told his mother the same day. In the evening I received a call from her, asking me to design the dome house.

What followed was another challenge. Nobody had ever built a dome house with the Hook&Build™ Building System. I designed the arches out of short straight pieces, interlocking them with the Hook&Build™ device to create an arch. This had not been done before either, and my structural engineer was excited about the opportunity to do something so new. He was convinced that the Hook&Build™ device would be strong enough, but he needed some proof that the device would hold up to all requirements. His computer could not handle this new situation. So we produced several testing samples, and tested them in a structural engineering lab. After reinforcing the Hook&Build™ device for this specific task, the structural engineer was satisfied with the results and we could carry on.

IN THE BEGINNING

The dome house is nearing completion. The system came together perfectly, every part fitted like a glove, and the framing structure was up in four days. Some pictures entitled Project Grande Prairie are included in this book.

Base of the Arch anchored to the Foundation Plate

Arches framed in horizontally for Roof Decking

Grand Prairie Project
Lower floor, showing the Floor Beams of the Main Floor

As I mentioned at the outset, my focus is to introduce this technology to everyone who is interested in it. There will be workshops for builders, contractors, and future home owners in a classroom setting and on the construction site. Classes will be given to architectural and engineering students, and presentations made to interested professionals in the construction industry (see: http://web.mac.com/wwilbert1).

The time is right for new ideas in the industry because:

1) The trade industry lacks expert trades people. Every year it becomes more difficult to find qualified people. Because of this shortage, prices go up and everything has to be done in a hurry to line up for the next job.

2) Energy saving is of great concern, because utilities are rising constantly. A tightly sealed home with a high insulation value is important.

3) Consumers are looking for a better return on investment. Traditional stick-build construction has a limited life expectancy. These days one is lucky if it lasts 50 to 60 years. More and more people ask if the home will last for generations, and if it will hold resale value.

4) Maintenance costs over a life span are another concern. Can improvements be done easily and cost efficient if the need arises?

5) Flexible floor plans are in demand. Can internal walls be changed when the family becomes larger or smaller?

These are just a few of the matters that need to be addressed in the housing industry.

IN THE BEGINNING

April 1, 2005

Writing this book, I received this information published at CNN International.com, World News.

Website:
http://edition.cnn.com/2005/WORLD/asiapcf/04/01/indonesia.earthquake.traditional.ap/index.html

This is more proof of the strength of post and beam structures.

Traditional houses outlast new houses in Indonesia quake

Everyone knows bricks are not so strong.

TUMORI, Indonesia (AP) -- You could call it the tale of two houses: one, a seemingly rickety stilt structure built 80 years ago using no nails stands defiantly upright, while next door, a six-year-old brick-and-cement home lies in a pile of rubble -- sent crashing to the ground by Monday's massive earthquake.

Friday, April 1, 2005 Posted: 1648 GMT (0048 HKT)
Residents stand around a traditional house at Gunung Sitoli in Nias island, Indonesia, Friday.

CONNECTIONS
LET'S HOOK&BUILD™

Connections

Developing the right beam connection hardware was not an easy task. Here are some of the more important qualities I was looking for:

1) The hardware should have the flexibility to make almost any beam connection possible.

2) It should be a locking-device, tying the connection together with great strength, so all parts become one component.

3) The device must be strong and ajustable in size and strength to fulfill all structural requirements in any situation.

4) It should be easy to install and easy and economical to produce.

5) It should be able to be made anywhere in the world.

SIMPLE POST & BEAM CONNECTIONS
(with horizontal beams)

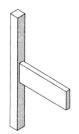

SINGLE BEAM CONNECTION TO POST

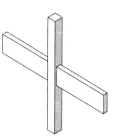

BEAM CONNECTION ON BOTH SIDES OF POST

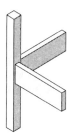

CORNER POST & TWO BEAM CONNECTIONS

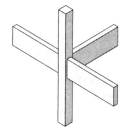

THREESIDED BEAM CONNECTION TO POST

BEAM TO BEAM CONNECTION

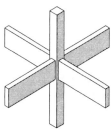

FOUR SIDED BEAM CONNECTION TO CENTER POST

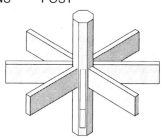

MULTIBLE BEAM CONNECTION TO ROUND CENTER POST

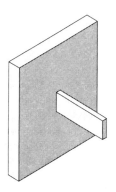

BEAM TO WALL CONNECTION

Connections

After inventing the Hook&Build™ Building System, I discovered to my surprise that there is hardly any situation where the Hook&Build™ device is unsuitable.

We had multiple connections where eight beams would meet in one location, building a hip-roof connection without a supporting post.

We also built a first time arch beam connection (never done before), where short beam sections are added to each other to create an arch.

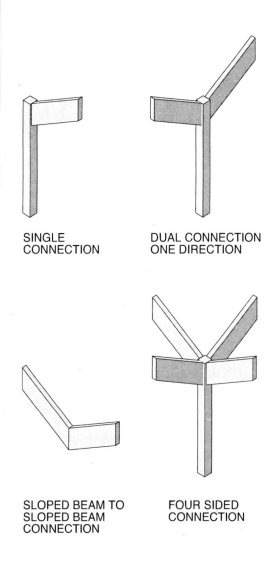

SINGLE CONNECTION

DUAL CONNECTION ONE DIRECTION

SLOPED BEAM TO SLOPED BEAM CONNECTION

FOUR SIDED CONNECTION

SIMPLE POST & BEAM CONNECTIONS
(sloped upwards beam)

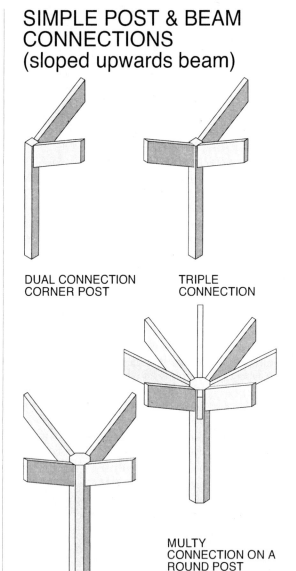

DUAL CONNECTION CORNER POST

TRIPLE CONNECTION

MULTY CONNECTION ON A ROUND POST

FOUR SIDED CONNECTION WITH A ROUND POST

Connections

Currently we use most often glue - laminated material for the post and beams, or a combination of steel and glue - laminated material.

Using steel posts with the Hook&Build™ hardware already welded in place makes for effortless installation of the frame of a 15,000 square foot building, three storeys high, in 7 1/2 days.

In the future we will add metals, pre-cast concrete, fiberglass, engineered wood, and in some situations, solid wood, to the framing materials.

SIMPLE POST & BEAM CONNECTIONS
(gable connections)

SINGLE CONNECTION

DUAL CONNECTION ONE DIRECTION

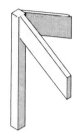
DUAL CONNECTION CORNER POST

TRIPLE CONNECTION

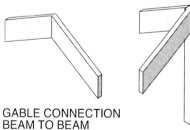
GABLE CONNECTION BEAM TO BEAM

FOUR SIDED CONNECTION

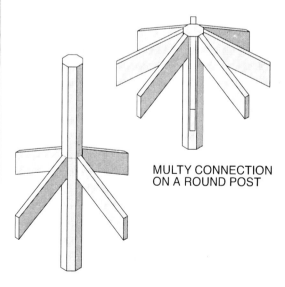
FOUR SIDED CONNECTION ON A ROUND POST

MULTY CONNECTION ON A ROUND POST

Connections

MULTY CONNECTIONS ON A TYPICAL PROJECT

Almost any type of building can be created with the Hook&Build™ Building System - your imagination is the limit. Ask twenty designers to create a 2,500 square-foot bungalow, and you will get 20 different designs and layouts.

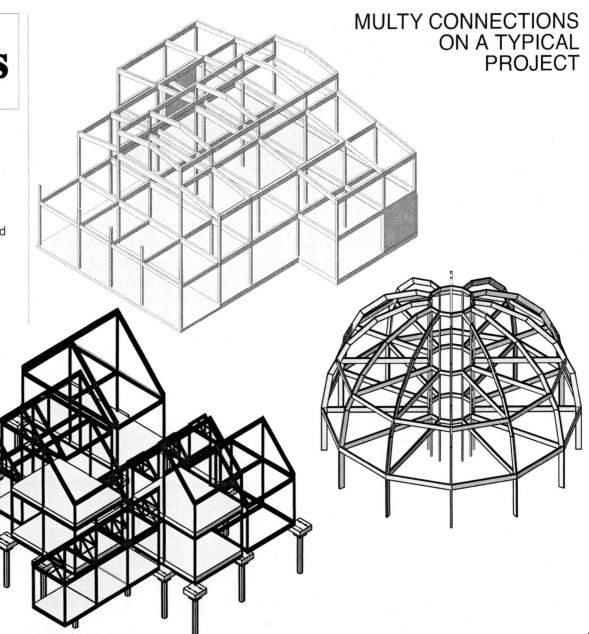

WHAT IS IT?
THE HOOK&BUILD™ BUILDING SYSTEM EXPLAINED

What is it?

• **Summary** •

The **Hook&Build™** Building System is a new and advanced post and beam construction technology like you never have seen before. The system uses a patented hardware device called the Hook&Build™ device, also called sometimes Wolfhook.

By using this device, the total framework of the post and beam structure is locked together with great strength and turns into a solid space frame. This space frame then becomes the structural carrier and guide of all other building components, including walls, floors, ceilings and roof systems, to complete the building.

The **Hook&Build™** Building System is completely pre-fabricated in the factory under high quality standards. Each part is quality checked, sprayed with a short time protective clear coating, wrapped for protection, and shipped to the building site. A ratchet wrench is then used by the installers to lock all components in place in short order.

The **Hook&Build™** device can adjust to any requirements, from a simple house to a mansion; from the street mall structure to a shopping centre; from a house built on piles in permafrost conditions; to a structure on a slope of a steep mountain, and from group housing to cluster installations. I am proud to make the Hook&Build™ Building System available worldwide to anyone in need of a safe and solid shelter.

What is it?

What are the Benefits of the Hook&Build™ Building System?

1) Affordable

I have seen many different construction technologies in my lifetime, and I had a personal involvement in many of them. When it comes to housing the variety of building methods is endless. It is amazing what is out there, from the sophisticated hightech structure to the man-made cave, from breathtaking dream homes to ugly boxes.

My intent was to provide you first of all with a safe and strong shelter to call home - a shelter that is unique to one's personal taste, a home that will last for several generations, and a home that is healthy, affordable and the best investment one can ever make.

Accordingly, the Hook&Build™ Building System is worth every cent and more. Where else could you get a completely engineered structural system, completely prefabricated, using one of the most beautiful materials in the industry, for such an economical price?

2) Effortless Installation

The assembly is perfect - neat and clean, like a piece of furniture. There is no measuring on the building site, no cutting or nailing involved, no wasted material. People respect the quality of the product and handle it with care. There are no hammer marks and improvised patch work. This is a post and beam frame one can be very proud of.

3) Expandable

Begin with a starter home and expand later. If the building site is large enough to allow additions to the home, this can be done easily with the "Hook&Build™" Building System. If the budget is tight, start with a smaller home, considering an expansion for the future. The beauty of the system is, that you can change or upgrade the look any time. Remember the post and beam frame is carrying the total structure.

Outside walls are like attachments or fill-ins; interior walls are partitions - none of them are bearing any weight of the structure.

4) Flexible Space and Shape

Open areas with no bearing walls means that interior walls can be relocated without compromising the integrity of the structural system. Changes in family size can be handled easily by changing, removing or adding wall units.

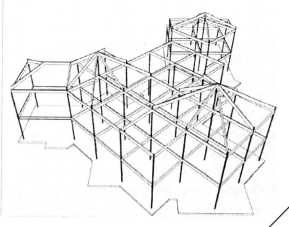

What is it?

5) Timeless Durability

.....that will last for generations. That cannot be said about other construction methods on the market. There is a certain natural principle on which the Hook&Build™ Building System is based. If you look at a human body, you will find a structural skeleton inside to carry the body, and a protective skin on the outside to protect the organs and the skeleton. One will find this combination in every animal, fish or bird. Even looking through a microscope you will find these two main elements in almost any physical structure. Have a closer look to see if other building types known follow this natural principle, and judge for yourself.

6) Difficult Locations

Slopes, rocks, permafrost ... any foundation will suit the Hook&Build™ Building System, whether slab, grade beam, basement or piles. Because of its interlocking system, the frame performs almost like a space frame. Added insulation panels as an outside skin will make this structure incredibly sturdy. Not every existing building method can follow the Hook&Build™ Building System on those difficult locations.

7) Earthquake Resistance

For financial reasons we cannot perform the table shake test yet to simulate an earthquake, but we have done tests in several university structural labs. The results show the Hook&Build™ Building System will be earthquake - resistant. Hopefully, in the near future, we will be able to perform this final test to prove the system's strength beyond doubt.

8) Higher R-Value

Adjustable thermal envelope. This is one of the biggest benefits of the Hook&Build™ Building System, it allows you to use almost any wall system you prefer. Most of the time the insulation panels are choosen for their high R-Values and their prefabricated nature. They are installed very quickly, and all that is needed, is to finish them on the exterior and interior.

Clients of mine used also straw bale walls as fill-ins in the frame structure. They are labor intensive, but provide an incredible R-Value and the sound proofing is amazing. Beside that, it creates a natural environment.

9) Material Savings

Up to 30% of saving in wood material. Post and beam construction is a very efficient technology in using wood materials.

What is it?

10) No Material Waste On Site

Off site prefabrication eliminates much of the wood that the stick build framing sends to the dumpster, or fire place. Our building sites are clean, with no cuttings, and no waste.

11) Unique

There is no system like it. The technology of the Hook&Build™ Building System is patented in North America and Japan, with patent pending internationally. It is available to everyone through the international distributor WW ENVIRONMENT TEAM LTD.

SUMMERIZING THE POINTS:

1) Affordable
(fast erection saves time and money)

2) Effortless Installation
(neat and clean assembly)

3) Expandable
(begin with a starter home and expand later)

4) Flexible Space and Shape
(open areas, no bearing walls)

5) Timeless Durability
(will last for many generations)

6) Difficult Locations
(easy erection on slopes, rocks, perma frost etc.)

7) Earthquake Resistance
(built solid like a rock)

8) Higher R-Value
(adjustable thermal envelope)

9) Saves Materials
(up to 30 per cent of saving in wood)

10) No Material Waste On Site
(off site prefabrication)

11) Unique
(nothing like it)

IMPORTANT TO KNOW:

The "Hook&Build™" Building System can be used with engineered timber such as glue-laminated material, Para Lam, Micro Lam, Tem Lam, Tech Lam and Box-Beams; also with metals, reinforced plastics, fiber glass and precast concrete. We welcome you to join us in the celebration of a new era in construction.

DESIGN
ALL THINGS CONSIDERED

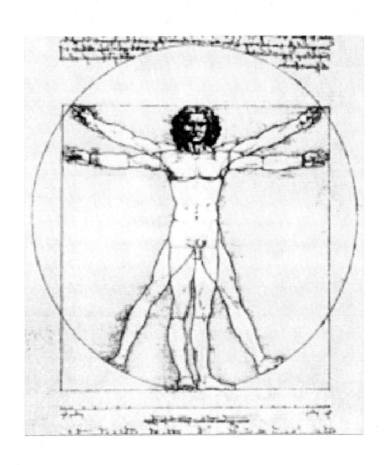

DESIGN

• General •

If you don't do it yourself, find the right professional person to design your home for you. Make sure this person understands your needs and has an excellent reputation as a designer and architect. Be sure to check references, talk to previous clients, and look at some of the projects this person has done in the past.

It is essential that your designer and you are on a common ground regarding the functionality of your new home, taste, style, form, material and color co-ordination. I always ask my clients to collect photographs and pictures out of magazines about the things they like and dislike. This is a good indicator for me if the client and I are complimenting each other in the process to design and build their new home. If this is not the case, it is better to bow out of the relationship before it creates hardship down the road for both parties.

Designing a new home is teamwork! It is the client who has to live in this new environment, it is he/she who has to feel comfortable and happy in his/her new house. The home is a reflection of the owner, and it should feel like both are made for each other.

The designer/architect has the vision and the imagination to bring the client's ideas to reality, by using his/her training, knowledge, experience, expertise. He is a professional guide in the process of making the client's dream a reality.

Certain steps in the designing stage are paramount.

Building Site

Before you start designing the house, have a close look at the building site:

- What is the orientation (north, south, east, west)?
- What is the main wind direction?
- Where are the possibilities to enter the property?
- What is the condition of the site (slope, bumpy, dry, wet, rocky, drainage)?
- What kind of vegetation is on the site (trees, shrubs)?
- What kind of neighborhood surrounds the property?
- Where are the utilities (water, electricity, gas, telephone)?
- Is there a water well, and if so, what is quality of the water?
- Is there a high or low water table?
- How is this building site under certain weather conditions and how does it perform during the different seasons?
- Where is the sunlight and where is the shade under different conditions?
- Are there underground natural water streems, and where are they located? Could they harm the energy? (If necessary, find a good dowser to help you with these questions).
- Is there a micro tower close by?
- Are there any high power lines?

DESIGN

Check with the city or county:

- Is there a lien on the property?
- What are the zoning and architectural requirements?
- Is there a height restriction?
- Are there any future developments planned for this area?
- Check out your neighbours as much as possible.
- Where are schools, hospitals, churches?
- What kind of transportation is available?

When a thorough understanding of the building site is accomplished, it is a good idea to talk to the neighbors about the weather conditions; did they have floods in their basements, are people in this area close and concerned about each other, or is everybody living an isolated life. Are there any people with building trade experience in your neighbourhood, and what is their reputation? Ask if your neighbours built there own homes, and what kind of experience they had, or if they used a general contractor, and how they rated his services.

Now that you have a clear picture of the situation, you can start thinking of your new home design.

These are just some general suggestions as to design procedure, but there is much more to it. The more you know, the better the result.

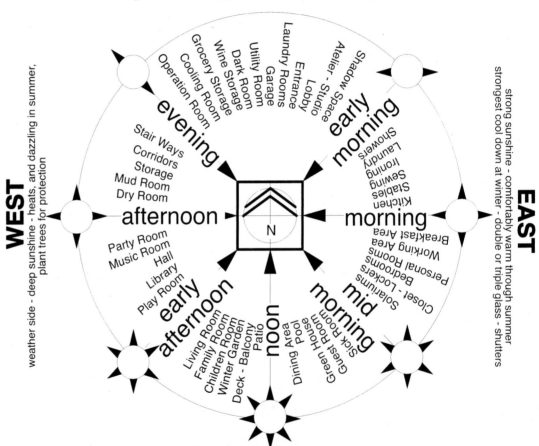

DESIGN

Outside walls become curtain walls, that are envelopes or skin enclosures to the structural frame. Interior walls become partitions, movable to almost any location fitting the requirements. As I mentioned before, I call this a natural structure, like the human body or any other animal protected by skin, scales, feathers or fur.

Even under the microscope one will find structures protected by some form of skin. This team of skeleton and skin has been proven in nature for eons. For this simple reason the Hook&Build Building System™
will outlast any stick built structure.

Designing a Post and Beam Home

There is a major difference in the principles of designing a post and beam Home compared to the traditional North American house design, in which the prefered method of construction is stick built framing.

Post and beam construction eliminates load bearing walls. The post and beam frame takes this responsibility, resulting in more flexibility. The open space allows the designer to be more innovative with the available floor space.

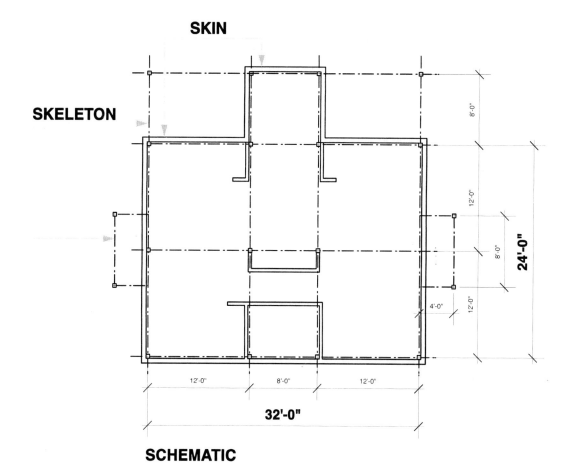

SCHEMATIC

DESIGN

There are many buildings in the market that do not follow this simple principle, and for that reason they have a limited life expectancy.

In this example of the SAMPLE HOME, I like to demonstrate how simple and easy a post and beam structure is. To the right is a simple small building with a footage of roughly 850 square feet (80 m2). Adding an attic second floor, increases the size of the building to 1,700 square feet (160 m2). The main floor is almost totally open, and only the bathroom is enclosed. No space is wasted on corridors, and there are only two posts in the centre of the house.

Please keep in mind that this is merely one for demonstration. The possibilities for designing a home are virtually endless.

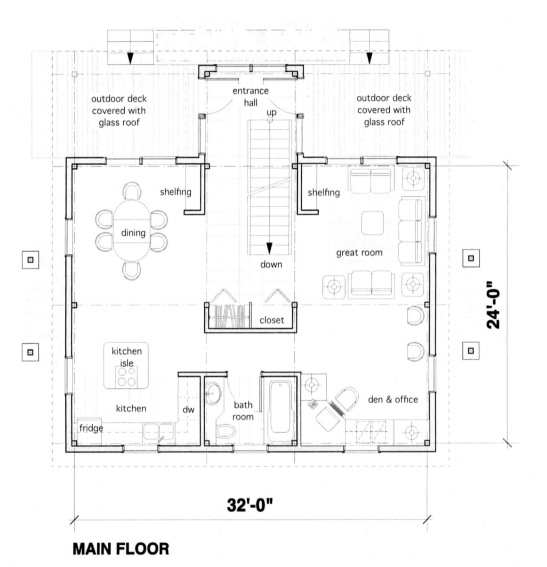

MAIN FLOOR

DESIGN

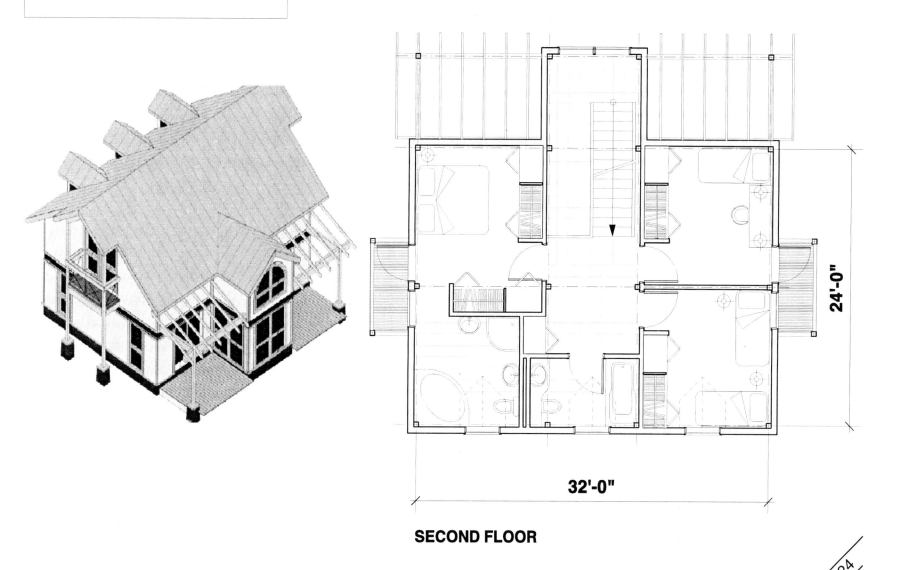

SECOND FLOOR

STEP BY STEP
SIMPLE INSTRUCTIONS TO START
WITH THE HOOK&BUILD™ BUILDING SYSTEM

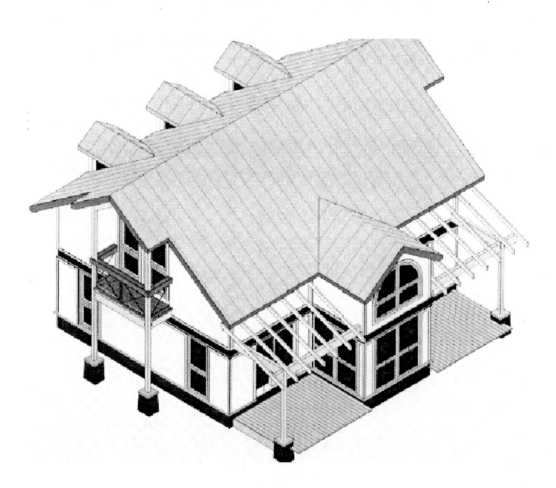

STEP BY STEP

Are you ready to receive the shipping of the "Hook&Build™" Building System?

First make sure you have the following in place:

1) When the shipment arrives, there should be people and/or equipment ready to unload the material. Depending on the size and weight of the items you have ordered, a forklift or similar equipment comes in handy.

Usually on smaller structures or frames where the master grid is not more then 10 to 12 feet, a few people can unload the framing by hand.

PLEASE FOLLOW THE UNLOADING INSTRUCTIONS CAREFULLY.

We will discuss the situation with our clients and suppliers beforehand, so you know what to expect.

What Tools are needed?

2) The most important tool to install the Hook&Build™ Building System, is a ratchet wrench. Actually, everyone on the installation team should carry one. Other wrenches as shown on the top are also helpful, but have more a secondary function. It can help to have some pliers handy; a rubber hammer if connections are very tight; also some tightening ropes and pulleys.

Fork Lift

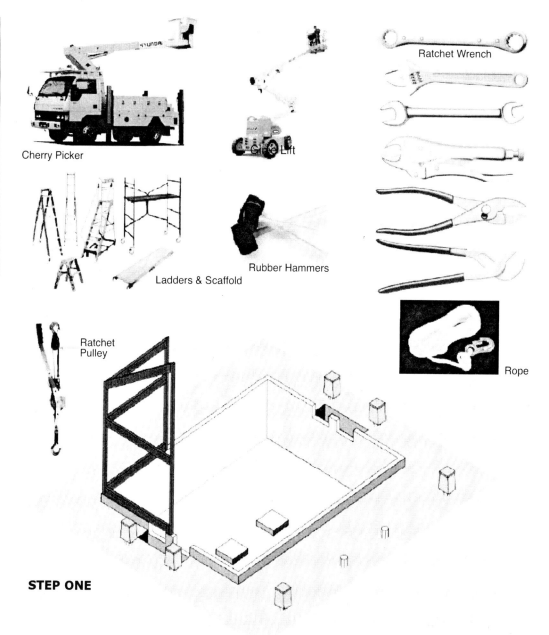

STEP ONE

STEP BY STEP

Never use a general hammer on the surface of the post and beam material! If you have to, protect the surface with a piece of clean wood, to make sure your post and beam material is not hammer marked.

You will need a crane or cherry picker to handle greater beam spans and larger buildings. A small Ginie Crane is also handy (as shown). This equipment saves time and improves security, allowing a building like this to go up in one to two days.

3) Each component has a sticker bearing a part number. These numbers correspond to the numbers in the shop drawings accompanying the rest of the building system.
Read and follow the instructions on the title sheet of these drawings.

4) Store the items on the building site on dry, level ground on top of some 4x4s, or similar boards. Create enough maneuvering and working space around the building site for you and your equipment. Store the items in groups of the same part numbers.

5) You have the most important tools and equipments in place, and you are ready to get started with the erection of the Hook&Build™ Building System.

6) Before we connect the beams and the posts together to create the framework, there is another important step to do.

Place the Hook&Build™ devices and the other hardware, like post anchors, first.

The only time this would not be necessary is when the posts are made from steel, and all the Hook&Build™ devices are already welded in the correct location.

7) When positioning the Hook&Build™ devices or any other hardware, open only the portion of the package involved with the hardware concerned. Leave the reminder of the post or beam material covered with the protective plastic. The wrapping will be removed when the frame is installed completely and ready for enclosure.

8) All the Hook&Build™ devices are placed ONLY on the POSTS. **This is important!** We use part numbers to fit the items correctly together. (Refer to the shop drawings for confirmation.) When the Hook&Build™ devices are lined up and centred, the bolts and nuts can be tightened up with solid strength.

Red Deer Project

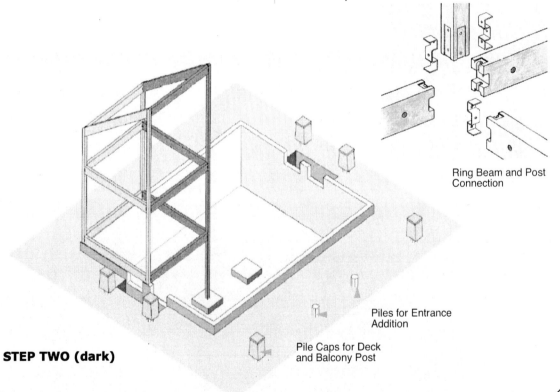

Ring Beam and Post Connection

Piles for Entrance Addition

Pile Caps for Deck and Balcony Post

STEP TWO (dark)

STEP BY STEP

Are all the Hook&Build™ devices and other hardware in place?

Make sure they are installed correctly and tightened up as well as possible!

The first step is perhaps the most difficult one. As you can see on the sketch (see Step 1), you will start on one corner of the foundation, usually the corner which would be the hardest to reach later in the process. The idea is to build a solid square of four posts (see Step 2). When this step is completed, you can tie up the connections firmly, but not too hard, because you may have to move the frame a fraction of an inch to line everything up correctly.

DO NOT ANCHOR THE POSTS TO THE FOUNDATION YET! THIS WILL BE DONE WHEN THE WHOLE FRAME IS UP AND LEVELED.

When the first square is completed with all the beams and rafter beams in place, it is relatively easy to work from this position towards the opposite site. For this example the erection of the total frame should not take any longer then two days.

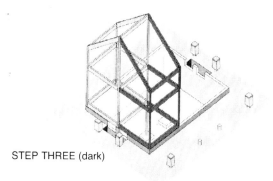

STEP THREE (dark)

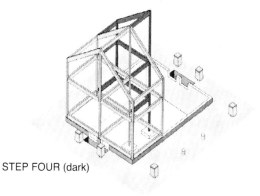

STEP FOUR (dark)

You have finished the first two steps successfully - the rest is easy from here. Just make sure you follow the steps as shown and the result will be perfect. The photographs on these pages illustrate projects ether in process or already done.

Morinville Project

Cochrane Project

Morinville Project

One point I need to stress: handle the frame system with care and respect. Just look at the superior material and the precise workmanship. This is NOT a stick build structure where you buy the lumber from a lumber yard, cut it on site and nail it together. Nobody really cares if the material gets dirty, stepped on or otherwise messed up, because it will be covered up and nobody will see it later anyway.

Be proud that you have something special and different. All the material is carefully selected and processed under quality control in the factory. The frame is professionally designed and engineered for you.

Computer technicians trained to produce accurate and easy to understand CAD shop drawings worked on the development of your frame.

STEP BY STEP

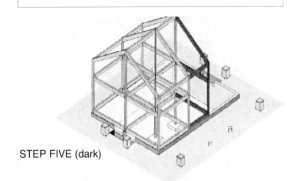

STEP FIVE (dark)

Highly trained experts, working with fully automated, million dollar equipment, programed these machines and watched the process of production.

The clear, protective coating is applied temporarily, to prevent dirt to penetrate into the wood during construction.

Then quality control takes over, checking that every single item produced is perfect and has the complete number of pieces.

Slave Lake Project

From there the items are numbered for identification and wrapped in protective plastic for transportation.

All you have to do is place the pieces together with your ratchet wrench.

Remember: your building will outlast the traditional North American construction method many times over. Your money is well invested, and you can be sure that your great - grandchildren will enjoy this special home.

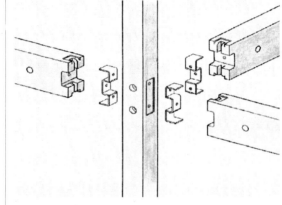

Side Post with three horizontal beams connected

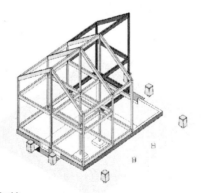

STEP SIX (dark)

Morinville Project

Cochrane Project

Calgary Project

STEP BY STEP

Morinville Project

Detail of four sided centre post with four horizontal beam connections

Alternate detail of two rafter beams supported by horizontal loading beam

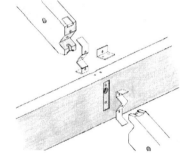

Detail of two rafter beams and two horizontal beams connecting to side post

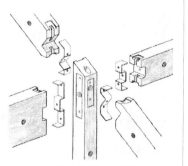

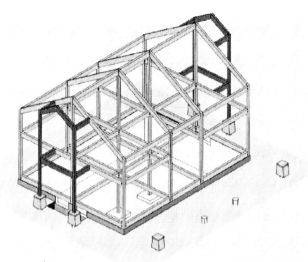
STEP EIGHT (dark)

Detail of side post and rafter beam connection

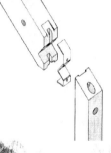

Parkland Project

Detail of alternate top rafter connection without post

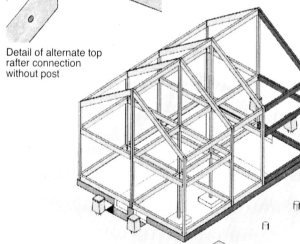
STEP SEVEN (dark)

STEP BY STEP

Sexsmith Project

Comox Project

Sexsmith Project

Morinville Project

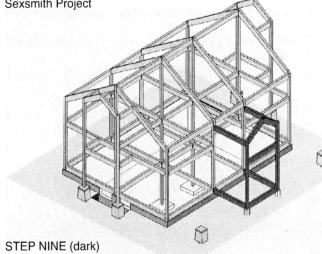
STEP NINE (dark)

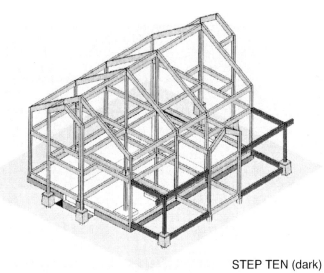
STEP TEN (dark)

Parkland Project

Calgary Project

Morinville Project

Slave Lake Project

THE FOUNDATION

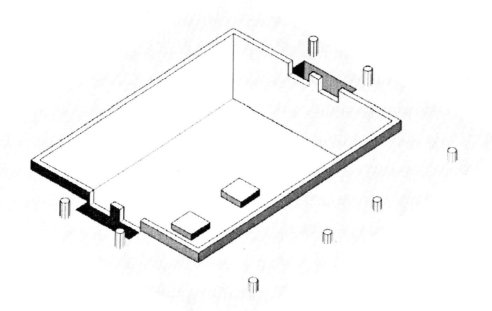

FOUNDATION

The Hook&Build™ Building System can be installed on whatever foundation is chosen based on the criteria formulated by the soil testing engineer and the structural engineer.

A very solid foundation connection can be accomplished with a ring beam system, where the beams are placed on top of a basement wall, grade beam, concrete slab or pile foundation. The ring beam follows the perimeter of the building, and is locked and connected to the outside posts of the structure to build a very tight ring on top of the foundation.

The post and beam frame also works without ring beams, by anchoring the posts with post anchors to the foundation. There are several ways to do this.

We have built the Hook&Build™ Building System on concrete slabs, basement walls, piles and grade beams with good results. The diagrams shown to the right illustrate how the Hook&Build™ Building System™ can be attached to those foundations.

I will not go into the technology of the different foundation details available as this is something the designer /architect or builder will decide, based on the recommendations of the structural engineer. There are also many books available in regards to foundations,

including:

- Graphic Guide to Frame Construction, by Rob Thallon
- Building Construction Illustrated, by Francis D.K. Ching

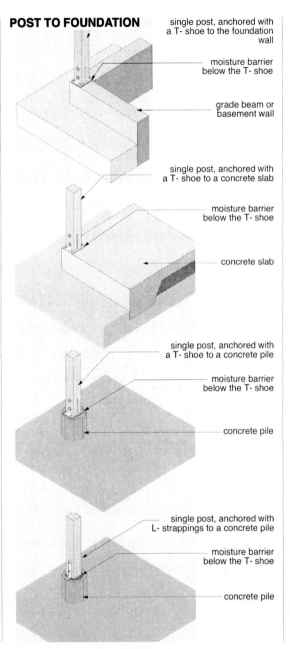

POST TO FOUNDATION

- single post, anchored with a T- shoe to the foundation wall
- moisture barrier below the T- shoe
- grade beam or basement wall
- single post, anchored with a T- shoe to a concrete slab
- moisture barrier below the T- shoe
- concrete slab
- single post, anchored with a T- shoe to a concrete pile
- moisture barrier below the T- shoe
- concrete pile
- single post, anchored with L- strappings to a concrete pile
- moisture barrier below the T- shoe
- concrete pile

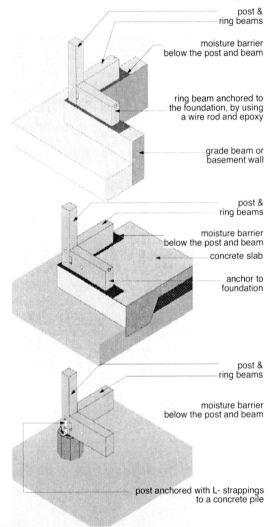

POST & RING BEAM TO FOUNDATION

- post & ring beams
- moisture barrier below the post and beam
- ring beam anchored to the foundation, by using a wire rod and epoxy
- grade beam or basement wall
- post & ring beams
- moisture barrier below the post and beam
- concrete slab
- anchor to foundation
- post & ring beams
- moisture barrier below the post and beam
- post anchored with L- strappings to a concrete pile

NOTE:

The above diagrams are only a few examples of the many possibilities. For other solutions please talk to your structural engineer or contractor or call the writer.

THE FLOOR SYSTEM

FLOOR SYSTEM

As with any construction, there are many ways to build a floor system. The Hook&Build™ Building System does not limit the numerous possibilities.

In our example, we will go with a traditional joist system. As you likely know, there are many options, including various joists - solid wood, plywood I joists, OSB I joists and laminated joists - as well as the floor trusses in different configurations (wood, wood/metal, metal). All of these can be used with the Hook&Build™ Building System.

The I-joist configuration (OSB or Plywood) is used often because it is economical, strong, engineered, silent and straight and accommodates long spans.

If height is restricted, we generally use metal hangers and place the joists between the beams of the Hook&Build™ Building System.

The best way however is to install the I-joists an top of the beams. From an optical view the beams are exposed on the level below, which then becomes a decorative part of the interior. The ceiling in this location is installed between the beams.

From a practical standpoint, the space between the I-joists becomes a utility area for the electrical, telephone, plumbing and heating systems. Your trades will love that because it makes their work so much easier. Without interruption one can basically run the utilities from one end of the building to the other. Sometimes trusses are even handier, because then utility lines can go in both directions.

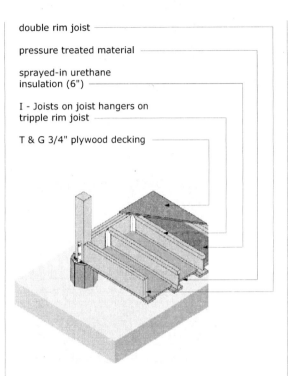

- double rim joist
- pressure treated material
- sprayed-in urethane insulation (6")
- I - Joists on joist hangers on tripple rim joist
- T & G 3/4" plywood decking

POST ON PILE

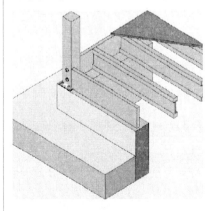

POST ON GRADE BEAM OR FOUNDATION

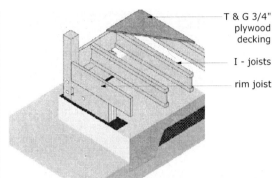

- T & G 3/4" plywood decking
- I - joists
- rim joist

POST & RING BEAM ON SLAB

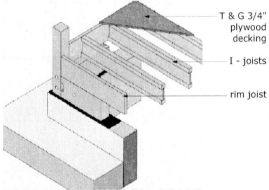

- T & G 3/4" plywood decking
- I - joists
- rim joist

POST & RING BEAM ON GRADE BEAM OR FOUNDATION

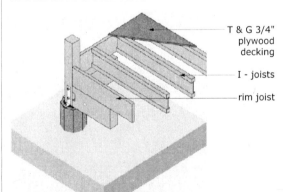

- T & G 3/4" plywood decking
- I - joists
- rim joist

POST & RING BEAM ON PILE

THE WALL SYSTEM

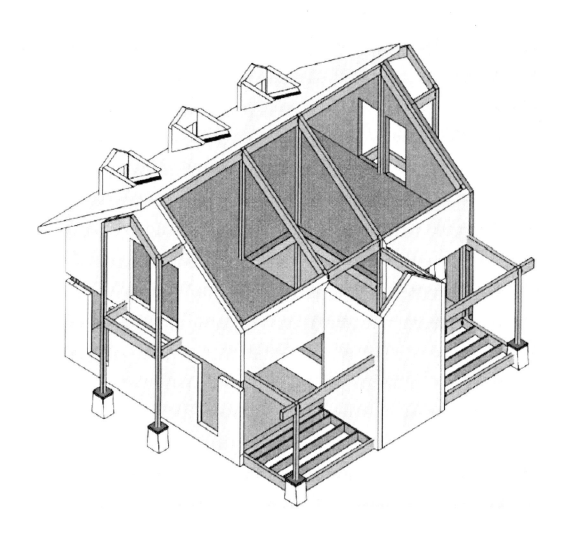

THE WALL

As mentioned before, the outside wall is not a bearing wall. The wall acts like a skin and is referred to as curtain wall or an in-fill.

The most popular wall system for post and beam structures (also called Timber Frames) is the insulation panel, also known as stress skin or structural panel. There is a difference between these panels. The insulation panel carries only its own weight and has to withstand some wind pressure and shear factors. The stress skin panel or structural panel is a completely engineered panel, designed to carry loads such as other floors and roofs, or large windows with great weights. Of course shear factors and wind and snow loads have to be considered as well. For this reason, the panel makers usually have engineers on staff to look after these requirements.

There are generally two types of insulation used in these panels: EPS (expanded polystyrene) also called Styrofoam, and polyurethane. Both products have their advantages and disadvantages, and are made from many different formulas. Check with the panel supplier about the mixture and make sure that the material has good fire resistance and the panels are completely cured, so that there is no more off-gassing after they are installed.

One of the great benefits of these panels is the insulation factor. Both products are excellent, the polyurethane insulation has a higher R-value, and a 6 1/2" panel reaches an R-value of R-40. The reason for the better performance is the greater density of the foam material.

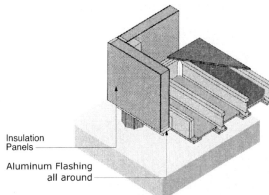

Insulation Panels
Aluminum Flashing all around

POST ON PILE

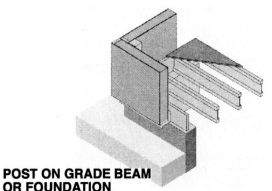

POST ON GRADE BEAM OR FOUNDATION

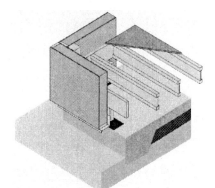

POST & RING BEAM ON SLAB

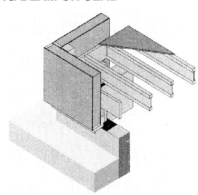

POST & RING BEAM ON GRADE BEAM OR FOUNDATION

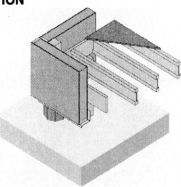

POST & RING BEAM PILE

THE WALL

Commox Project

In the fabrication process both products are made differently. The EPS material comes to the panel makers in specified sizes and thicknesses to be laminated with in and outside sheeting (usually OSB boards 3/8" to 1/2" thick). To make sure the thickness of the panel is continuous, and the glue connection permanent, a large hydraulic press is used in the final process.

In comparison, the polyurethane insulation is injected in hollow wall panels, held in place by a huge hydraulic press. Most of the time the injection of the expanding foam is done on one side of the panel, and when the foam appears on the other side of the panel, through very tiny holes, the panel is usually filled.

To be absolutely sure that all installed panels are completely filled with insulation, an infrared photograph of the heated house on a cool day will show yellow to red colors where the leakages are. A blue picture shows a very airtight house.

We have used both panel types and we were satisfied with the performance of both of them. The polyurethane insulation can also be sprayed on the building side if a panel maker is not easily available at the building location.

These panels are an ideal combination to the Hook&Build™ Building System. Both systems are prefabricated in factories, and structurally engineered. Using a glue-laminated post and beam system guarantees also that the frame is absolutely straight and perfectly aligned for the panel installation. Because of that, the panel installer never has to be concerned about bent, cracked and twisted timber. Shrinkage of the frame during the drying process is also eliminated. This means a quick installation, and in case of our example of the SweetHome, the panels are erected in one day.

TERMAL SPLINE CONNECTIONS

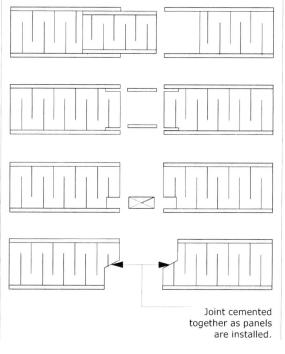

Joint cemented together as panels are installed.

The panels can be directly installed to the frame by using rust free, long screws and silicone sealers for joints. Usually, if there is a grade beam, foundation wall or concrete slab, we leave a lip or saddle of 1 1/2" to 3" deep for an easy start up.

Before this is done a flashing has to be placed to stop driving rain water going to the bottom of the panel. We recommend that the solid wood on the bottom edge of the panel is made from pressure treated wood.

Calgary Project

Insulation panels are typically made from 7/16" to 1/2" OSB boards for standard outside and inside skin.

The insulation material is usally EPS styrofoam or polyurethane.

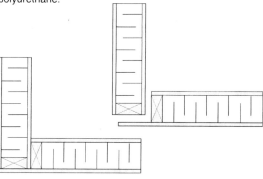

Alternate Corner Connection

THE WALL

STRAW BALE

The straw bale builders are excited about the Hook&Build™ Building System. For them it is a perfect solution because the straw bales are not loaded with the weight of the roof system. Straw bales have to be tightened and pre-compressed Kentucky style to avoid any major settling later. Similar to log construction, the final settling can leave gaps inches wide.

The most serious threats to straw bale construction are moisture and rain. Wet bales start to mold in the core, and a wet bale already installed has to be replaced. In fact, water is almost more damaging then fire, especially when the building is already built.

There are six criteria straw balers love about the Hook&Build™ Building System:

1) The installed supporting frame works like a guideline in regards to alignment and leveling.

2) All window and door frames can be attached to the framing.

3) There are no diagonal bracings in the way; the in-fills are square.

4) The weight of the roof structure is not loaded on the bales; they only have to carry their own weight.

Cochrane Project

5) Most important, the Hook&Build™ Building System can be installed complete with the finished roof. The straw bales can be stored in the centre of the building, protected completely from any moisture or rain. They can actually sit there and dry out completely before installation.

6) The dimensions of the frame can complement the sizes of the bales, so the fittings and cuttings can be reduced to a minimum.

In some ways, straw bale construction can be labor intensive if the working crew is not experienced. As simple as it seems, there are certain rules essential to making the process successful. On the back of the book I refer to experienced and excellent straw bale designers and installers in Western Canada.

On the other hand, a well made straw bale house has wonderful qualities. It is a natural structure, and the quality of air and comfort is awesome. Besides an incredible R-value, deep interior window sills, round and smooth corners, the soundproofing is fantastic.

Cochrane Project

I understand there are straw bale buildings that are centuries old and still occupied.

THE ROOF SYSTEM

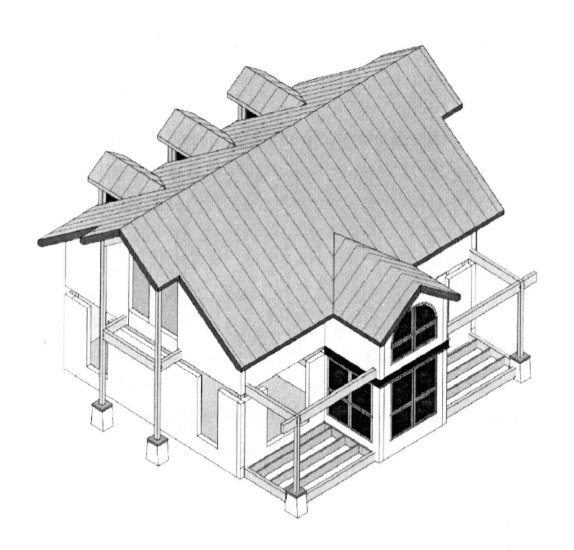

THE ROOF

PANEL ROOF SYSTEM

Similar to the wall system, there are also roof insulation panels available. Because warm air travels up, the roof should have the highest R-value factor. A R-40 rating is usually recommended.

To calculate the right structural panel for the roof, the engineer needs to know several facts:

1) distance between supports to carry the size of the panel
2) degree of roof slope
3) the snow loads in this location
4) wind loads and shear factors

Knowing these conditions, the structural engineer will design the needed reinforcement for the roof panel.

An insulated panel roof is often a "warm" roof -as opposed to a "cold" roof where you have a constant airflow between the insulation and the actual roof skin (attic).

If the roof panel permits, a roof system that allows an airspace between the insulation panel and the final roof skin is preferable. Many practical ideas in this regard are published.

The roof can also be done with traditional solid roof joists or I-joist systems.

Prefabricated roof trusses can also be used, especially if the roof is shallow, or an open cathedral ceiling is not possible or desired.

Prefabricated roof trusses come in many shapes: king post truss, mono pitch fruss, fink truss, scissors and parallel chord trusses.

Parkland Project

The Hook&Build™ Building System simply stops at the roof line, providing a supporting beam in this location to carry the load of the roof trusses.

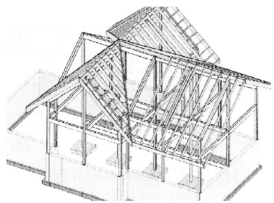
Morinville Project

Parkland Project

This book is not designed to get into further details about roof structures. Please refer to information specific to this field.

FINISHING THE OUTSIDE

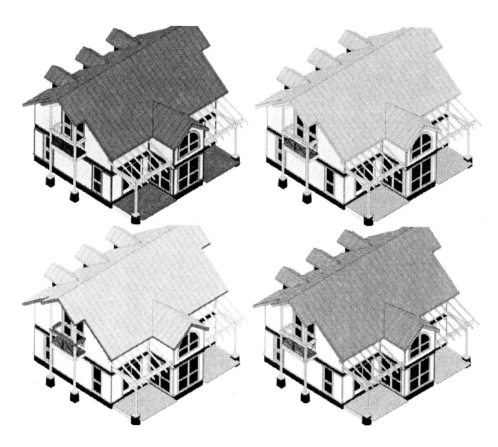

FINISHING

FINISHING THE OUTSIDE

Using insulation panels for the outside walls, opens a whole array of possibilities as to the finished look of the home.

Similar to the stick-build structure, the raw panel skin is made from OSB (Open Strand Board), plywood or similar materials.

All available sidings - wood, wood cement, wood shingles, fibre, vinyl, metal - can be applied easily.

Other finishing styles are stucco, brick or stone cladding (real or artificial), and cement tiles.

It is advisable to create an airspace for ventilation behind the final skin. During the rain season, trapped moisture between skin and panel can then dry out easily. On hot summer days the siding cools off quickly because of the airflow effect.

DIFFERENT FACADES AND FINISHING MATERIALS

DETAILS
NOW IT MAKES SENSE

This part of the book shows some typical building details relating to foundations, wall sections and roof sections.

The intention is to provide suggestions for the designer, to help with the process of the working drawings, and to convey a greater understanding of how easily all components of the building fit together.

The Hook&Build™ Building System is truly a guideline and template for every building component that follows. Mistakes are easily avoided during the construction process because the Hook&Build™ Building System outlines all dimensions in all directions, and is square and leveled from the beginning.

Details

The standard basement wall consists of simple basics.

There is an H&B ring beam sitting on top of the wall, tightened to the H&B posts and anchored with wire rods to the foundation wall. The wire rods are dipped on one end in epoxy, and then pushed into the prepared holes in the basement wall. The epoxy will cure in the concrete, and after that the ring beam will be locked into place with a washer and tie-nut.

The floor system is made from I - joists and is placed together with the rim - joist on top of the H&B ring beam.

This solution allows all utilities to run in the floor - joist space, making utility installation easy.

Insulation panels used for the outside envelope and bolted with special screws to the framing.

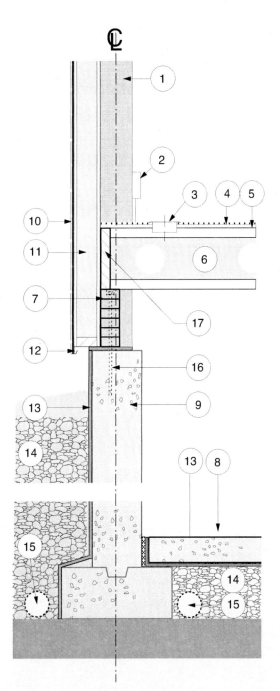

STANDARD BASEMENT WALL
NOTE: H&B stands for Hook&Build™

1) H&B Glue - Lam Post (fir, pine or spruce)
2) Power outlet service mounted on each column 6" to 12" over finished floor
3) Heating register installed at window locations (if forced air heating is used)
4) Floor finish
5) T&G floor sheathing (5/8" or 3/4")
6) I-Joist 16" o.c., or as otherwise as specified by the engineer.
7) H&B glue - lam Beam
8) Concrete slab
9) Concrete basement wall
10) Outside finishes (siding, stucco, brick veneer etc.)
11) Prefabricated stress-skin panel (insulated)
12) Aluminum flashing (continuous)
13) Protective membrane / waterproofing
14) Sand and Gravel
15) Continuous perforated drainpipe (inside optional)
16) Wire rod anchor through glue-lam beam into foundation wall
17) Rim joist

Details

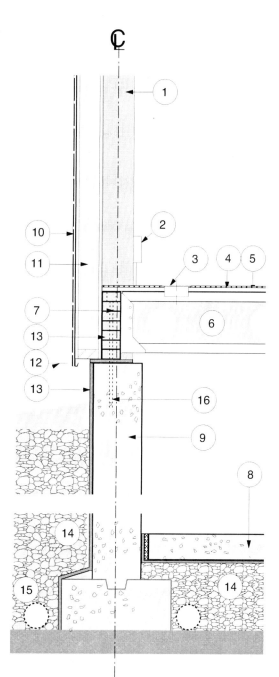

STANDARD BASEMENT WALL / 2
NOTE: H&B stands for Hook&Build™

This wall section is identical with the basement wall section previously shown. The only difference is that the floor-joists are **not** sitting on the top of the H&B ring beam; they are now placed with hangers between the H&B glue-lam beams.

This solution is used if the height of the building is restricted, or costs must be cut in building materials. However, this usually does not pay off, because the extra and more complicated work for the installation of the utilities will take up any savings.

1) H&B glue - lam post (fir, pine or spruce)
2) Power outlet service mounted on each column 6" to 12" over finished floor
3) Heating register installed at window locations (if forced air heating is used)
4) Floor finish
5) T&G floor sheathing (5/8" or 3/4")
6) I-Joist 16" o.c., or as otherwise specified by the engineer.
7) H&B glue - lam beam
8) Concrete slab
9) Concrete basement wall
10) Outside finishes (siding, stucco, brick veneer)
11) Prefabricated stress - skin panel (insulated)
12) Aluminum flashing (continuous)
13) Protective membrane / waterproofing
14) Sand and gravel
15) Continuous perforated drainpipe (inside optional)
16) Wire rod anchor through glue - lam beam into foundation wall

Details

Often people want a quiet floor system, where you don't hear every step from the upper floor.

Sometimes it is a question of how can one have a heating system with some radiating effects.

A concrete subfloor can do both very well. Using the subfloor also as the carrier of the floor heating system makes it a radiating storage mass.

Even when the heating is turned off, the heated concrete subfloor will deliver warmth for hours.

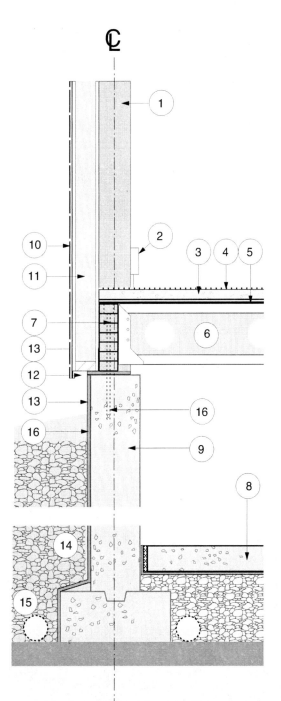

CONCRETE SUB-FLOOR
NOTE: H&B stands for Hook&Build™

1) H&B glue - lam post (fir, pine or spruce)
2) Power outlet service mounted on each column 6" to 12" over finished floor
3) Concrete subfloor 1 1/2" to 2" thick
4) Floor finish
5) T&G floor sheathing (5/8" or 3/4")
6) I-Joist 16" o.c., or as specified by the engineer.
7) H&B glue - lam beam (ring beam)
8) Concrete slab
9) Concrete basement wall
10) Outside finishes (siding, stucco, brick veneer etc.)
11) Prefabricated stress - skin panel (insulated)
12) Aluminum flashing (continuous)
13) Protective membrane / waterproofing
14) Sand and gravel
15) Continuous perforated drainpipe
    inside optional)
    Wire rod anchor through glue - lam beam into foundation wall

Details

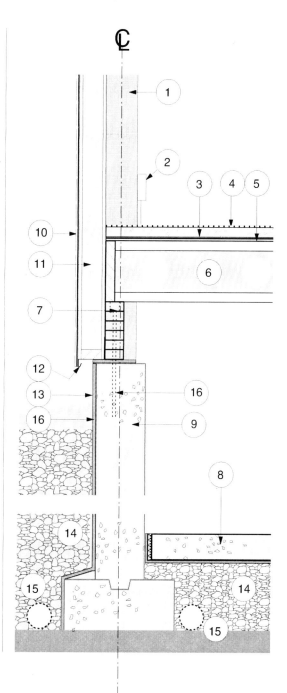

CONCRETE SUB-FLOOR/2
NOTE: H&B stands for Hook&Build™

1) H&B glue - lam post (fir, pine or spruce)
2) Power outlet service mounted on each column 6" to 12" over finished floor
3) Concrete subfloor 1 1/2" to 2" thick
4) Floor finish
5) T&G floor sheathing (5/8" or 3/4")
6) I-Joist 16" o.c., or as specified by the engineer.
7) H&B glue - lam beam (ring beam)
8) Concrete slab
9) Concrete basement wall
10) Outside finishes (siding, stucco, brick veneer etc.)
11) Prefabricated stress - skin panel (insulated)
12) Aluminum flashing (continuous)
13) Protective membrane / waterproofing
14) Sand and gravel
15) Continuous perforated drainpipe (inside optional)
16) Wire rod anchor through glue - lam beam into foundation wall

With this subfloor solution the floor system is found on top of the ring beam.

As previously mentioned, this concept is especially preferable for the installation of utilities (heating, plumbing, power, telephone).

The space provided in the floor system makes installation of a floor heating so much easier.

Details

Sometimes a simple foundation system is used - in this case a pile foundation.

Reasons for using it include a high water table, permafrost condition, unstable ground, cost consideration or other site requirements.

Piles can be made from timber, concrete or steel. They can be visible, providing openly air circulation, or be hidden and enclosed with a pony wall, providing still an air circulation through a calculated vent system.

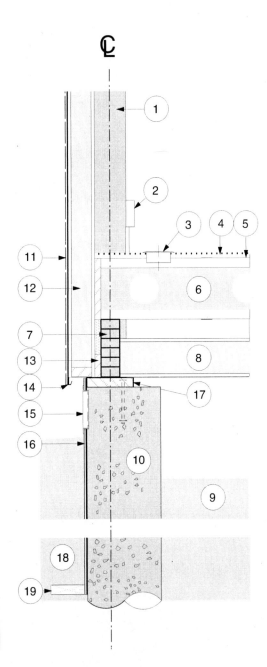

BUILDING ON PILE FOUNDATION

NOTE: H&B stands for Hook&Build™

1) H&B glue - lam post (pine or spruce) 5" x 5"
2) Power outlet service
3) Heating register installed at window locations
4) Floor finish
5) T&G floor sheathing (5/8" or 3/4")
6) Joist 16" o.c., or as specified by the structural engineer
7) H&B glue - lam beam
8) Insulated floor panel (stress skin)
9) Sand and gravel fill
10) Concrete pile 12" diam. 16'-0" deep, reinforced with four #4 rebars 16'-0" deep, or as specified by the structural engineer
11) Finished siding panels
    Alternate: fine stucco
12) Prefabricated stress - skin panel (insulated)
13) Spacer board
14) Aluminum flashing (continuous)
15) Vent
16) Pressure treated plywood 4' x 8' x 5/8" screwed to edger plate
17) Ledger plate pressure treated 1 1/2" x 7 1/2", anchored with 1/2" anchor bolt 7-8" long
18) Sand and Gravel
19) Pressure treated 2" x 6"

Details

The interior H&B post basically has the same detail features as the outside post. Besides that a higher load is carried by this post; it can be hidden away in interior partitions; or it becomes an obvious feature in the design of the interior.

In this case we decided to have the floor system sitting on top of the H&B beams, so the beams are also an element of the ceiling design. The exposed H&B beams are bringing architectural character, warms and optical strength to the interior space.

The ceiling is installed beween the H&B beams, and because the floor system is above the H&B beams, there is plenty of room for indirect lighting, and sound speakers.

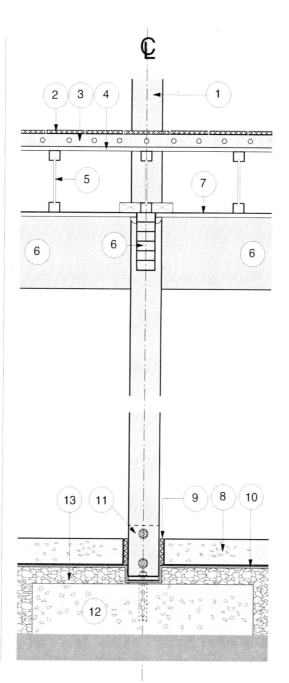

THE INTERIOR POST
NOTE: H&B stands for Hook&Build™

1) H&B glue - lam post (fir, pine or spruce)
2) Finished floor (ceramic tiles or similar)
3) Subfloor concrete with integrated heating system
4) T&G floor sheathing (5/8" or 3/4")
5) Joist 16" o.c. or as specified by engineer
6) H&B glue - lam beam
7) Ceiling (gypsum board, ceiling tiles, paneling etc.)
8) Concrete slab
9) Expansion joint
10) Concrete rated moisture barrier
11) Post anchor welded steel, upside down "T" shape, fitting size of post, bolted twice through post, and anchored to concrete foundation plate
12) Concrete foundation plate (size specified by engineer)
13) Sand and gravel fill compacted

Details

There are many ways to design grade beams. The detail to the right is only one of many possibilities. They come in different sizes and shapes, and their specific design relies on location, soil condition, and of course the type of weather it is exposed to.

Some locations have greater earth movement then others, especially if there is heavy vegetation close to the building, or if there are frozen ground conditions.

Also technical elements can play a role; for example if the floor is heated by coils (water/electrical) or by forced air.

Heat loss is another concern. For this reason the slab and grade beam should be protected by rigid insulation and not exposed to the cold.

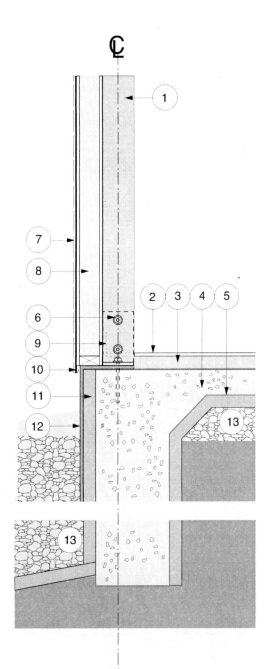

THE GRADE BEAM FOUNDATION

NOTE: H&B stands for Hook&Build™

1) H&B glue - lam post (fir, pine or spruce)
2) Finished floor (ceramic tiles or similar)
3) Subfloor concrete with integrated heating system
4) Concrete slab
5) Concrete rated moisture barrier and 1 1/2" to 2" rigid insulation
6) Post anchor welded steel, upside down "T" shape, fitting size of post, bolted twice through post, and anchored to concrete foundation plate and grade beam (size specified by engineer)
7) Wall finish outside (siding, stucco, brick veneer)
8) Insulated wall panel
9) Base board (hidden)
10) Continuous metal flashing (Alum)
11) Rigid insulation 1 1/2" to 2"
12) Protective shield material (fibre board)
13) Sand and gravel fill compacted

Details

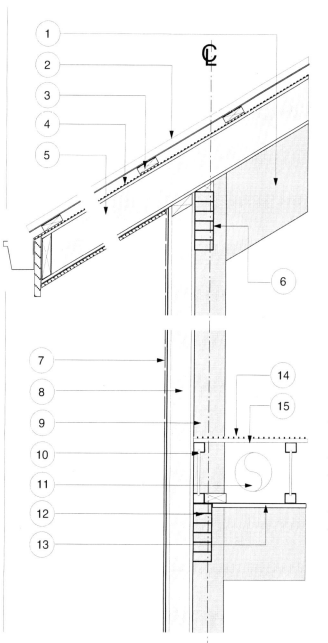

USING ROOF INSULATION PANELS

NOTE: H&B stands for Hook&Build™

1) H&B glue - lam rafter beam (fir, pine or spruce)
2) Finished roof
3) Roof strapping for air circulation
4) Air space
5) Roof insulation panel
6) H&B horizontal glue - lam beam
7) Wall finish outside (siding, stucco, brick veneer)
8) Insulated wall panel
9) H&B glue - lam post
10) Joist 16" o.c. or as specified by the engineer
11) Utility space for heating, electrical, plumbing
12) Horizontal glue - lam beam
13) Ceiling (gypsum board, ceiling tiles, paneling)
14) Finished floor
15) T&G floor sheathing (5/8" or 3/4")

If open cadethral ceilings are desired, the open post and beam construction of the "Hook&Build™" Building System easily fulfills these requirements.

Together with insulated stress skin roof panels, this task is very economical and efficient, and a R-value of R-40 can be achieved easily.

Details

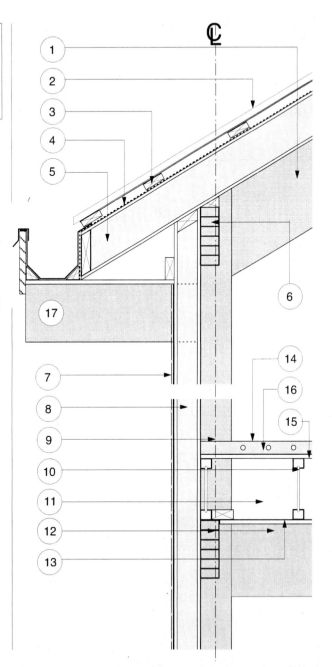

As in the previous details, this building section shows another cathedral ceiling with a different design of roof overhang; also the floor system is slightly different - a light concrete subfloor with a floor heating system is used.

All these details can be altered or combined with each other, depending on the needs for the particular project.

Again insulation panels are used for the wall and roof system.

ALTERNATE CATHEDRAL CEILING CHOICE

NOTE: H&B stands for Hook&Build™

1) H&B glue - lam rafter beam (fir, pine or spruce)
2) Finished roof
3) Roof strapping for air circulation
4) Air space
5) Roof insulation panel
6) H&B horizontal glue - lam beam
7) Wall finish outside (siding, stucco, brick veneer)
8) Insulated wall panel
9) H&B glue - lam post
10) Joist 16" o.c. or as specified by the engineer
11) Utility space for heating, electrical, plumbing.
12) H&B horizontal glue - lam beam
13) Ceiling (gypsum board, ceiling tiles, paneling)
14) Finished floor
15) T&G floor sheathing (5/8" or 3/4")
16) Light concrete sub - floor
17) H&B deco beam

Details

This detail shows a cathedral ceiling with a different design of roof overhang.

All these details can be altered or combined with one other, depending on the needs for the particular project.

Again insulation panels are used for the wall and roof system.

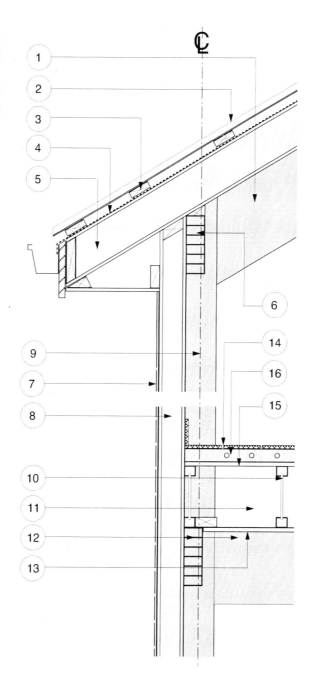

ALTERNATE CATHEDRAL CEILING CHOICE

NOTE: H&B stands for Hook&Build™

1) H&B glue - lam rafter beam (fir, pine or spruce)
2) Finished roof
3) Roof strapping for air circulation
4) Air space
5) Roof insulation panel
6) H&B horizontal glue - lam beam
7) Wall finish outside (siding, stucco, brick veneer)
8) Insulated wall panel
9) H&B glue - lam post
10) Joist 16" o.c. or as specified by the engineer
11) Utility space for heating, electrical, plumbing
12) H&B horizontal glue - lam beam
13) Ceiling (gypsum board, ceiling tiles, paneling)
14) Finished floor
15) T&G floor sheathing (5/8" or 3/4")
16) Light concrete sub - floor

Details

Again another cathedral ceiling with a different design for the roof overhang....

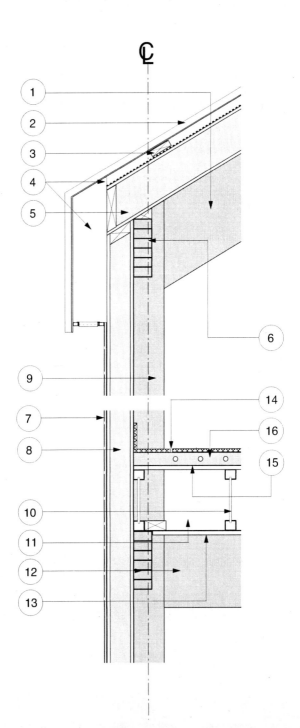

ALTERNATE CATHEDRAL CEILING CHOICE

NOTE: H&B stands for Hook&Build™

1) H&B glue - lam rafter beam (fir, pine or spruce)
2) Finished roof
3) Roof strapping for air circulation
4) Air space
5) Roof insulation panel
6) H&B horizontal glue - lam beam
7) Wall finish outside (siding, stucco, brick veneer)
8) Insulated wall panel
9) H&B glue - lam post
10) Joist 16" o.c. or as specified by the engineer
11) Utility space for heating, electrical, plumbing
12) H&B horizontal glue - lam beam
13) Ceiling (gypsum board, ceiling tiles, paneling)
14) Finished floor
15) T&G floor sheathing (5/8" or 3/4")
16) Light concrete sub - floor

Details

Another cathedral ceiling with a different design of roof overhang......

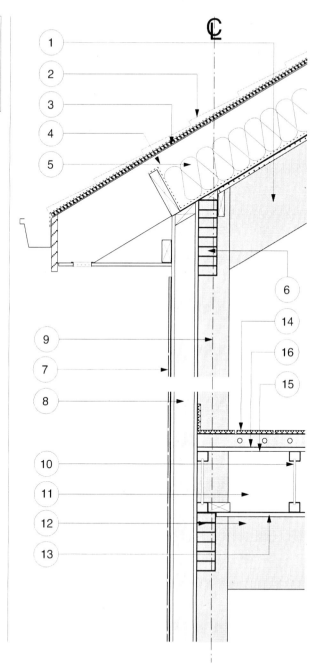

ALTERNATE CATHEDRAL CEILING CHOICE

NOTE: H&B stands for Hook&Build ™

1) H&B glue - lam rafter beam (fir, pine or spruce)
2) Finished roof
3) Roof sheathing (plywood, OSB) roofing paper
4) Air Space
5) Butt insulation (R-40)
6) H&B horizontal glue - lam beam
7) Wall finish outside (siding, stucco, brick veneer)
8) Insulated wall panel
9) H&B glue - lam post
10) Joist 16" o.c. or as specified by the engineer
11) Utility space for heating, electrical, plumbing
12) H&B horizontal glue - lam beam
13) Ceiling (gypsum board, ceiling tiles, paneling)
14) Finished floor
15) T&G floor sheathing (5/8" or 3/4")
16) Light concrete sub - floor

Details

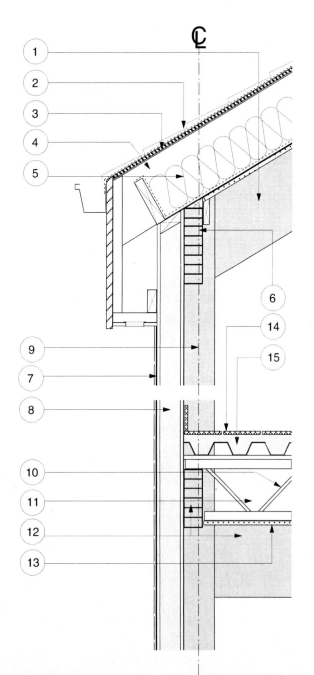

This detail shows another cathedral ceiling with a different design of roof overhang.

See also an alternate floor system, using a steel joist system and steel decking.

ALTERNATE CATHEDRAL CEILING CHOICE

NOTE: H&B stands for Hook&Build™

1) H&B glue - lam rafter beam (fir, pine or spruce)
2) Finished roof
3) Roof sheathing (plywood, OSB), roofing paper
4) Air space
5) Butt insulation (R-40)
6) H&B horizontal glue - lam beam
7) Wall finish outside (siding, stucco, brick veneer)
8) Insulated wall panel
9) H&B glue - lam post
10) Steel joist 16" o.c. or as specified by the engineer
11) Utility space for heating, electrical, plumbing
12) H&B horizontal glue - lam beam
13) Ceiling (gypsum board, ceiling tiles, paneling)
14) Finished floor
15) Steel deck with concrete sub - floor

Details

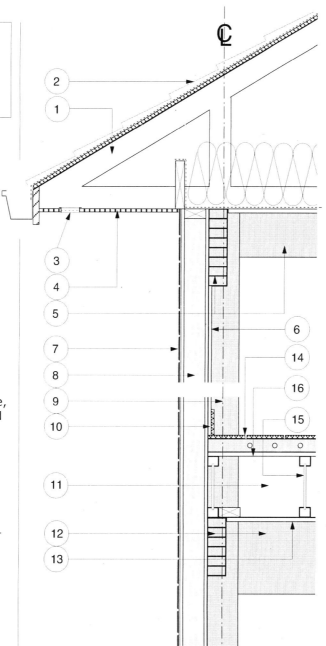

POST & BEAM & PREFABRICATED ROOF TRUSSES

NOTE: H&B stands for Hook&Build™

Prefabricated roof trusses are perfect in combination with the H&B post and beam system, especially, if a cold roof approach (ventilated) is prefered over the insulation panel, and if a cathedral ceiling is not important.

These roof trusses can be built in any shape, overhang and slope. They are simply placed on the H&B top ring beam similar to a Stick-Built outside wall for support.

1) Prefabricated roof truss
2) Finished roof
3) Roof vent
4) Soffit
5) H&B horizontal glue - lam beam
6) Finished interior wall
7) Wall finish outside (siding, stucco, brick veneer)
8) Insulated wall panel
9) H&B glue - lam post
10) Base board
11) Utility space for heating, electrical, plumbing
12) H&B horizontal glue - lam beam
13) Ceiling (gypsum board, ceiling tiles, paneling)
14) Finished floor
15) I-Joist floor system 16" o.c., or as otherwise specified by the structural engineer
16) T&G floor sheathing (5/8" or 3/4")

Details

POST & BEAM & PREFABRICATED ROOF TRUSSES

NOTE: H&B stands for Hook&Build™

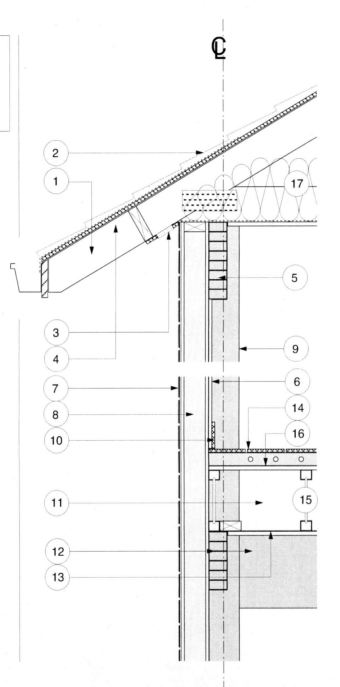

ALTERNATE ROOF TRUSS

Different prefabricated roof trusses continued with the H&B post and beam system.

1) Prefabricated roof truss
2) Finished roof
3) Roof vent
4) Soffit
5) H&B horizontal glue - lam beam
6) Finished interior wall
7) Wall finish outside (siding, stucco, brick veneer)
8) Insulated wall panel
9) H&B glue - lam post
10) Baseboard
11) Utility space for heating, electrical, plumbing
12) H&B horizontal glue - lam beam
13) Ceiling (gypsum board, ceiling tiles, paneling)
14) Finished floor
15) I-Joist floor system 16" o.c., or as otherwise
    specified by the structural engineer
16) T&G floor sheathing (5/8" or 3/4"), light crete sub - floor (1 1/2" -2"), with floor heating
17) Roof insulation

Details

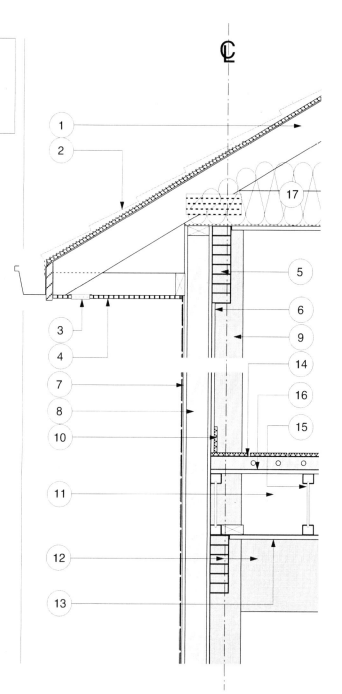

POST & BEAM & PREFABRICATED ROOF TRUSSES

NOTE: H&B stands for Hook&Build™

1) Prefabricated roof truss
2) Finished roof
3) Roof vent
4) Soffit
5) H&B horizontal glue - lam beam
6) Finished interior wall
7) Wall finish outside (siding, stucco, brick veneer)
8) Insulated wall panel
9) H&B glue - lam post
10) Baseboard
11) Utility space for heating, electrical, plumbing.
12) H&B Horizontal glue - lam beam
13) Ceiling (gypsum board, ceiling tiles, paneling)
14) Finished floor
15) I-joist floor system 16" o.c., or as otherwise
    specified by the structural engineer
16) T&G floor sheathing (5/8" or 3/4"), light - crete sub - floor (1 1/2" -2"), with floor heating
17) Roof insulation

ALTERNATE ROOF TRUSS

Different prefabricated roof trusses continued with the H&B post and beam system.

Details

This view shows another way to simplify the roof structure without using any roof overhang, while retaining the cathedral effect on the second floor.

This concept would also have industrial and commercial applications.

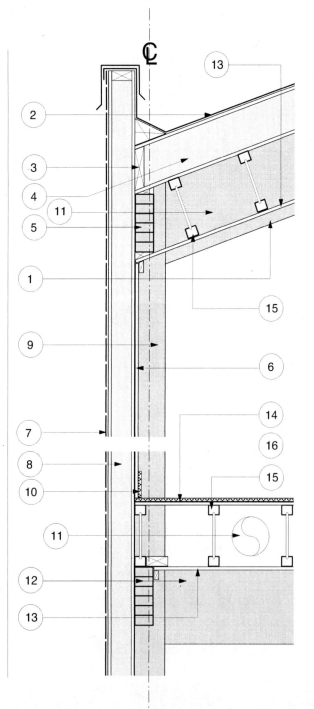

DIFFERENT ROOF APPROACH

NOTE: H&B stands for Hook&Build™

1) H&B glue - lam rafter beam (fir, pine or spruce)
2) Finished roof (2-Ply or hot air welded)
3) Solid edge for insulation roof panel
4) Insulation roof panel minimum R-40
5) H&B horizontal glue - lam beam
6) Finished interior wall
7) Wall finish outside (siding, stucco, brick veneer)
8) Insulated wall panel
9) H&B glue - lam post
10) Baseboard
11) Utility space for heating, electrical, plumbing
12) H&B horizontal glue - lam beam
13) Ceiling (gypsum board, ceiling tiles, paneling)
14) Finished floor
15) I-joist floor system 16" o.c., or as otherwise specified by the structural engineer
16) T&G floor sheathing (5/8" or 3/4")

Details

A similar approach was shown on page #61. The difference here, is that the roof joists are not between the rafter beams but on top of it. This way an extra mechanical / utility space is created.

This is another way to simplify the roof structure, without using any roof overhang. The Cathedral effect is retained on the second floor.

This concept would also have industrial and commercial applications.

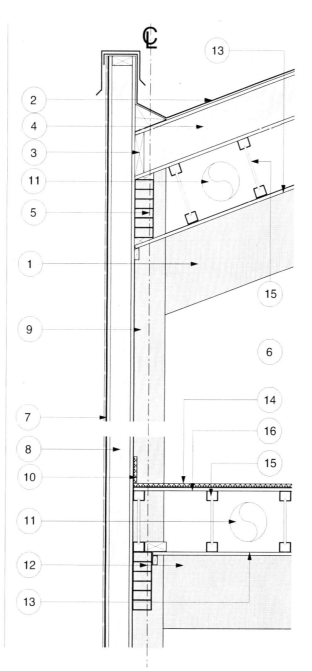

DIFFERENT ROOF APPROACH

NOTE: H&B stands for Hook&Build™

1) H&B glue - lam rafter beam (fir, pine or spruce)
2) Finished roof (2-Ply or hot air welded)
3) Solid edge for insulation roof panel
4) Insulation roof panel min. R-40
5) H&B horizontal glue - lam beam
6) Finished interior wall
7) Wall finish outside (siding, stucco, brick veneer)
8) Insulated wall panel
9) H&B glue - lam post
10) Baseboard
11) Utility space for heating, electrical, plumbing
12) H&B horizontal glue - lam beam
13) Ceiling (gypsum board, ceiling tiles, paneling)
14) Finished floor
15) I-joist floor system 16" o.c., or as otherwise specified by the structural engineer
16) T&G floor sheathing (5/8" or 3/4")

Details

ALTERNATE ROOF TRUSS

Different prefabricated roof trusses continued with the H&B post and beam system.

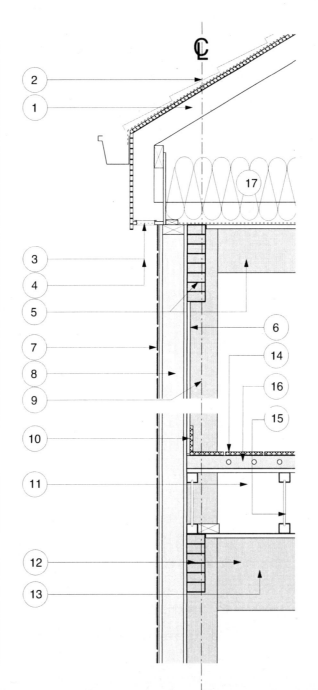

POST & BEAM & PREFABRICATED ROOF TRUSSES

NOTE: H&B stands for Hook&Build™

1) Prefabricated roof truss
2) Finished roof
3) Roof vent
4) Soffit
5) H&B horizontal glue - lam beam
6) Finished interior wall
7) Wall finish outside (siding, stucco, brick veneer)
8) Insulated wall panel
9) H&B glue - lam post
10) Baseboard
11) Utility space for heating, electrical, plumbing
12) H&B horizontal glue - lam beam
13) Ceiling (gypsum board, ceiling tiles, paneling)
14) Finished floor
15) I-joist floor system 16" o.c., or as otherwise specified by the structural engineer
16) T&G Floor sheathing (5/8" or 3/4")
17) Roof insulation

Details

The design of a simple flat roof system is efficient and installation friendly with the Hook&Build™ Building System.

The possibilities of using different standard roof and floor systems are incredible.

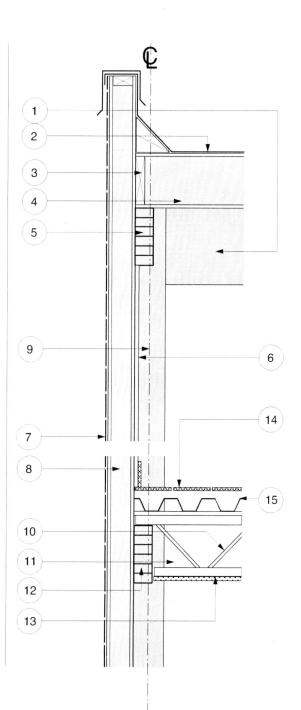

FLAT ROOF CONSTRUCTION WITH INSULATION PANEL

NOTE: H&B stands for Hook&Build™

1) H&B glue - lam roof beam (fir, pine or spruce)
2) Finished roof (2-ply or hot air welded)
3) Solid edge for insulation roof panel
4) Insulation roof panel minimum R-40
5) H&B horizontal glue - lam beam
6) Finished interior wall
7) Wall finish outside (siding, stucco, brick veneer)
8) Insulated wall panel
9) H&B glue - lam post
10) Steel joist specified by engineer
11) Utility space for heating, electrical, plumbing
12) H&B horizontal glue - lam beam
13) Ceiling (gypsum board, ceiling tiles, paneling)
14) Finished floor
15) Steel deck with concrete sub - floor

Details

This view shows another use of flat roof construction.

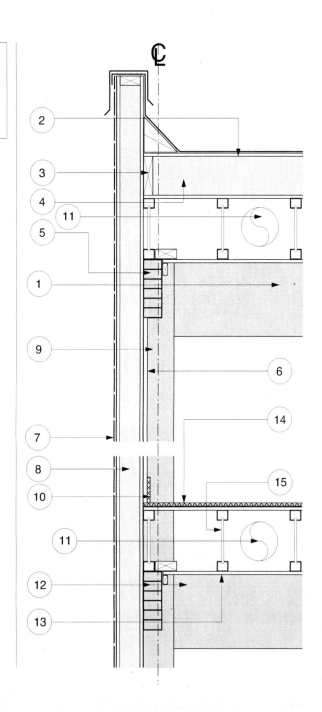

FLAT ROOF CONSTRUCTION WITH INSULATION PANELS

NOTE: H&B stands for Hook&Build™

1) H&B glue - lam roof beam (fir, pine or spruce)
2) Finished roof (2-ply or hot air welded)
3) Solid edge for insulation roof panel
4) Insulation roof panel minimum R-40
5) H&B horizontal glue - lam beam
6) Finished interior wall
7) Wall finish outside (siding, stucco, brick veneer)
8) Insulated wall panel
9) H&B glue - lam post
10) Baseboard
11) Utility space for heating, electrical, plumbing
12) H&B horizontal glue - lam beam
13) Ceiling (gypsum board, ceiling tiles, paneling)
14) Finished floor
15) I-joist floor system 16" o.c., or as otherwise specified by the structural engineer

Details

In this view I-joists support insulated roof panels and provide utility space by exposing the post & beam structure to the interior.

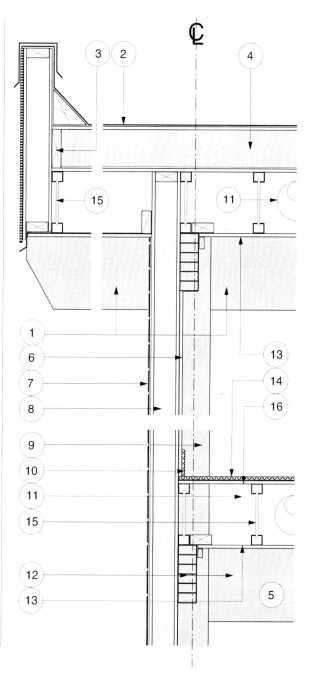

FLAT ROOF APPLICATION

NOTE: H&B stands for Hook&Build™

1) H&B glue - lam roof beam (fir, pine or spruce)
2) Finished roof (2-ply or hot air welded)
3) Solid edge for insulation roof panel
4) Insulation roof panel minimum R-40
5) H&B horizontal glue - lam beam
6) Finished interior wall
7) Wall finish outside (siding, stucco, brick veneer)
8) Insulated wall panel
9) H&B glue - lam post
10) Baseboard
11) Utility space for heating, electrical, plumbing
12) H&B horizontal glue - lam beam
13) Ceiling (gypsum board, ceiling tiles, paneling)
14) Finished floor
15) I-joist floor system 16" o.c., or as otherwise specified by the structural engineer
16) T&G floor sheathing (5/8" or 3/4")

Details

This application demonstrates the flexibility of the Hook&Build™ Building System.

An economical post and beam framing system is used for the structure which is completed with a truss roofing system.

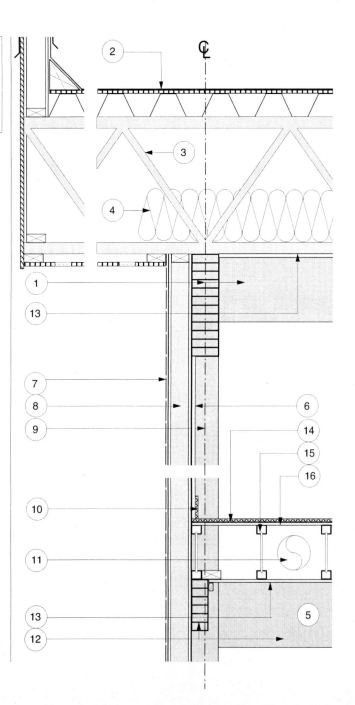

INDUSTRIAL & COMMERCIAL APPLICATIONS

NOTE: H&B stands for Hook&Build™

1) H&B glue - lam roof beam (fir, pine or spruce)
2) Finished roof (2-ply or hot air welded)
3) Industrial roof trusses
4) Insulation roof minimum R-40, vapor barrier as by Building Code
5) Horizontal glue - lam beam
6) Finished interior wall
7) Wall finish outside (siding, stucco, brick veneer)
8) Insulated wall panel
9) Glue - lam post
10) Baseboard
11) Utility space for heating, electrical, plumbing
12) H&B horizontal glue - lam beam
13) Ceiling (gypsum board, ceiling tiles, paneling)
14) Finished floor
15) I-joist floor system 16" o.c., or as otherwise specified by structural the engineer
16) T&G floor sheathing (5/8" or 3/4")

Details

POST & BEAM & STRAW BALE

NOTE: H&B stands for Hook&Build™

Straw Bale construction has been around for a long time. Many publications and articles have been written about this unique construction system.

Clients used the Hook&Build™ Building System in the past as a structural carrier for the straw bale walls.

Because of the very fast erection of the Hook&Build™ Building System, and the easy installment of a roof system, straw bales can be stored under the roof and kept dry, which is a very important requirement for safe straw bale construction. The framework also allows easy integration of window and door systems, and there are no bracings in the way of erecting the straw bale walls.

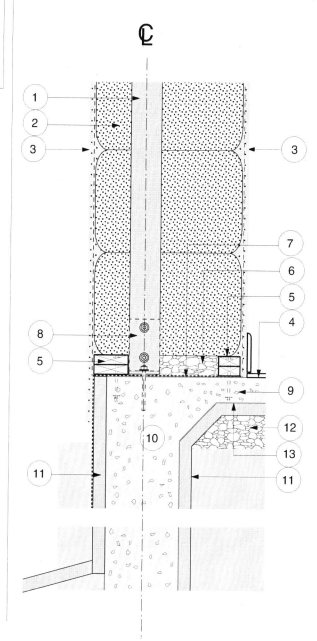

1) H&B glue - lam post (pine or spruce) 5" x 5" hidden in the straw bale wall
2) Straw bales, interconnected vertically with long bamboo sticks
3) Heavy stucco cover made from natural sources like clay, or in combination with concrete mixtures.
4) Floor finish
5) Pressure treated base frame, anchored to the Concrete Slab or Grade Beam.
6) Fill-in gravel mixed with sand, absorbing any moisture to keep bales dry.
7) Moisture barrier between base frame and concrete
8) Post steel anchor (T-shaped)
9) Concrete slab
10) Grade beam
11) Rigid insulation 1 1/2" to 2" thick.
12) Compacted gravel and sand
13) Moisture barrier preventing moisture to the concrete slab

Details

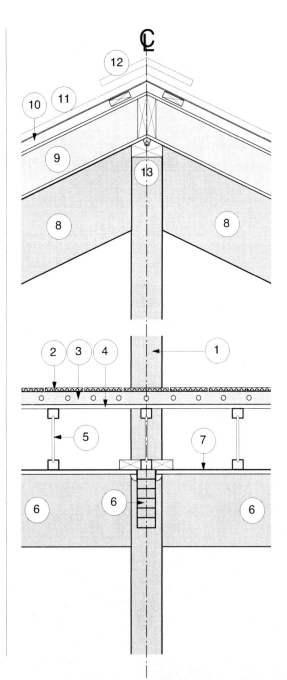

The gable detail can have a H&B centre post, as shown in this layout, with the related floor system example below.

A insulated Stress Skin Panel Roof with metal roofing material is used. Rafter beams are exposed to the interior to create a cathedral ceiling.

Using this H&B framing solution, allows also for other roof systems, like for instance ventilated roof systems with extra joist support, and traditional insulation systems.

THE INTERIOR POST & ROOF GABLE

NOTE: H&B stands for Hook&Build™

1) H&B glue - lam post (fir, pine or spruce)
2) Finished floor (ceramic tiles or similar)
3) Subfloor concrete with integrated heating coil
4) T&G floor sheathing (5/8" or 3/4")
5) Joist 16" o.c. or as specified by the engineer
6) H&B glue - lam beam
7) Ceiling (gypsum board, ceiling tiles, paneling)
8) H&B rafter beam
9) Insulation roof panels
10) Ventilation space
11) Roofing material
12) Roofing vent
13) Trim with hidden electric cable

Details

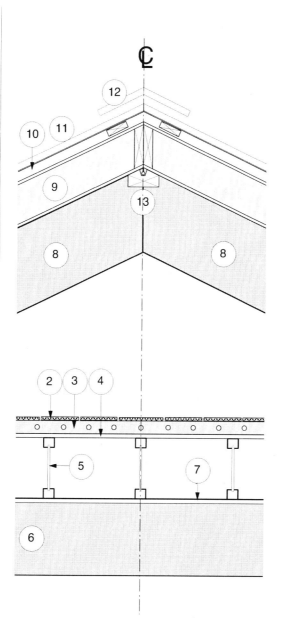

Here is the gable detail without the centre post (as shown on the previous page). Both H&B rafter beams come together on the gable point and are locked together with the Hook&Build™ hardware.

Otherwise, the concept is identical to that shown on page 69.

THE ROOF GABLE

NOTE: H&B stands for Hook&Build™

2) Finished floor (ceramic tiles or similar)
3) Subfloor concrete with integrated heating coil
4) T&G floor sheathing (5/8" or 3/4")
5) Joist 16" o.c. or as specified by the engineer
6) H&B glue - lam beam
7) Ceiling (gypsum board, ceiling tiles, paneling)
8) H&B rafter beam
9) Insulation roof panels
10) Ventilation space
11) Roofing material
12) Roofing vent
13) Trim with hidden electric cable

Details

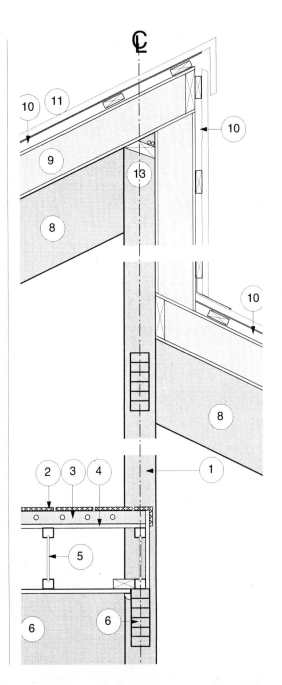

In this roof detail we show another possible use of the Hook&Build™ Building System.

This is just one example - almost any shape and form can be built with the H&B Building System, from a dome structure to a pyramid - shaped building. The only limit is your imagination.

THE INTERIOR POST & RAFTER BEAMS

NOTE: H&B stands for Hook&Build™

1) H&B glue - lam post (fir, pine or spruce)
2) Finished floor (ceramic tiles or similar)
3) Subfloor concrete with integrated heating coil
4) T&G floor sheathing (5/8" or 3/4")
5) Joist 16" o.c. or as specified by the engineer
6) H&B glue - lam beam
7) Ceiling (drywall, ceiling tiles, paneling)
8) H&B rafter beam
9) Insulation roof panels
10) Ventilation space
11) Roofing material
12) Trim with hidden electric cable

Details

Sometimes clients prefer that the exposed ends of the beams be shaped in a decorative way to enhance the character of the building.

Here are a few of the examples of what can be used for this purpose.

DECO BEAMS

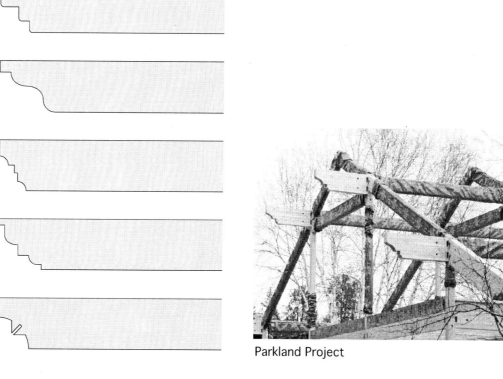

Parkland Project

Details

Bracings are found mostly in the timber frame construction. They are first of all stiffeners for the framing itself, but sometimes double as a finishing detail or decoration.

In any case, they come in all forms and shapes, as the picture below demonstrates.

The drawings to the right were used in one of our projects.

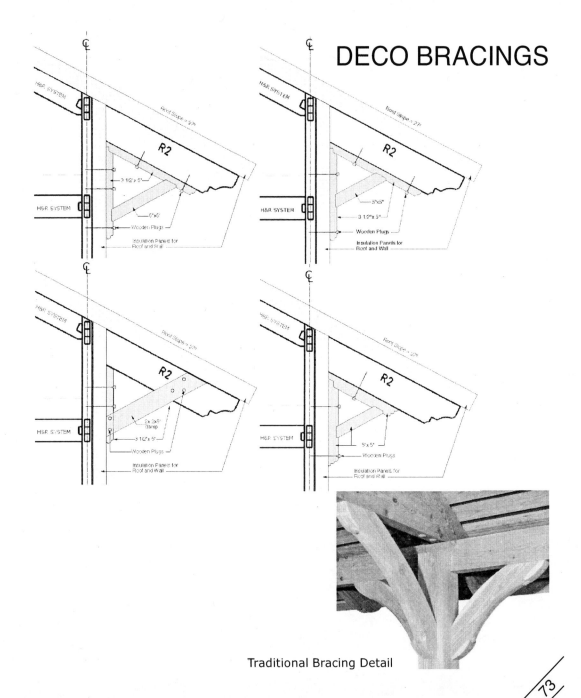

DECO BRACINGS

Traditional Bracing Detail

EMERGENCY
IN DISASTER ZONES

EMERGENCY CONCEPTS

NEW ORLEANS MODULAR SHELTER
Sept. 2, 2005

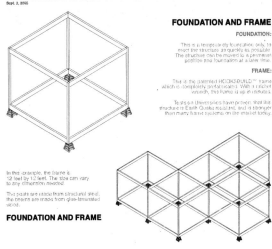

FOUNDATION AND FRAME

FOUNDATION:
This is a temporary foundation only, to erect the structure as quickly as possible. The structure can be moved to a permanent position and foundation at a later time.

FRAME:
This is the patented HOOK&BUILD™ frame which is completely prefabricated. With a ratchet wrench, this frame is up in minutes.

Tests on Universities have proven, that this structure is Earth Quake resistant, and is stronger then many frame systems on the market today.

In this example, the frame is 12 feet by 12 feet. The size can vary to any dimension needed.

The posts are made from structural steel, the beams are made from glue-laminated wood.

FOUNDATION AND FRAME

INSULATED FLOOR PANEL

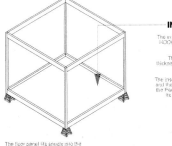

The Insulated Floor Panel is placed right after the HOOK&BUILD™ Frame is installed, leveled and locked into position.

The Insulated Floor Panel can have different thicknesses, depending on the R-value needed in certain areas.

The insulation panel is carrying only its own weight, and therefore does not have to be structural. After the Panel is in place, sealing and caulking around its perimeter is required to make the panel air tight.

The floor panel fits snugly into the 12 feet by 12 feet Floor Beam Frame.

It can be made from EPS, or from Polyurethane. The thickness of the Panel depends on the R-Value requirements in the area.

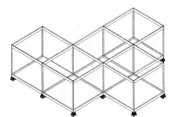

MULTY MODULAR UNITS

INSULATED ROOF PANEL

The Insulated Roof Panel is placed on top of the HOOK&BUILD™ Frame, covering the Frame from outside edge to outside edge.

The Insulated Roof Panel can have different in thicknesses, depending on the R-value needed in this areas.

The insulation panel is a structural panel, and it strength has to be calculated on the rain/snow load in this location.

After the Panel is in place, sealing and caulking around it perimeter is required to make the panel air tight.

The Roof Panel fits from edge to edge of the HOOK&BUILD™ Frame.

It can be made from EPS, or from Polyurethane. The thickness of the Panel depends on the R-Value requirements in the area.

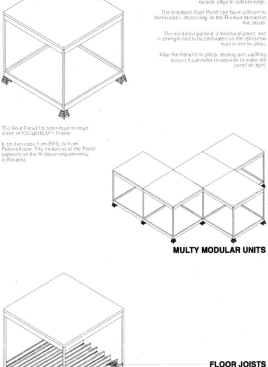

MULTY MODULAR UNITS

FLOOR JOISTS

Floor Joists are placed on top of the Ring Floor Beam. They can be made from solid wood, engineered wood like I-Joists (as shown), Metal 'C' joists or equal.

The Floor Joists placed on top of the Floor Ring Beams, creates a plenum space between the insulated Floor Panel below and the T&G Floor sheeting.

This space can be utilized for heating, cooling, plumbing and other utilities.

MULTY MODULAR UNITS

T&G FLOOR SHEETING

The T&G Sheeting is the base floor for any floor finishing desired, depending on the use of space.

The Floor Sheeting can be made by different materials, depending on the availability or economic.

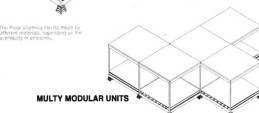

MULTY MODULAR UNITS

WINDOWS & DOORS

The Windows & Doors can be made in any size or material desired. For extra protection against break-ins, high winds, rain storms ect., extra window & door shutters can be installed.

Wall finish on the inside could be painted gypsum board or equal. Any siding (vinyl, wood, metal etc.) or stucco can be used for the finishing outside.

FINISH WITH ONE PLY ROOFING SYSTEM

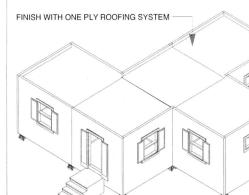

PREFABRICATED STAIR SYSTEM

cut-out pages of a study

75

EMERGENCY CONCEPTS

NEW ORLEANS MODULAR SHELTER
Sept. 2, 2005

WINDOWS & DOORS

The Windows & Doors can be made in any size or material desired. For extra protection against break-ins, high winds, rain storms ect., extra window & door shutters can be installed.

Wall finish on the inside could be painted, gypson board or equal. Any siding (vinyl, wood, metall etc.) or stucco can be used for the finishing outside.

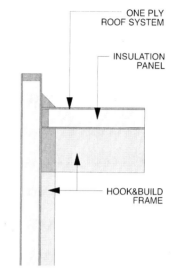

- FINISH WITH ONE PLY ROOFING SYSTEM
- PREFABRICATED STAIR SYSTEM

MULTY MODULAR UNITS

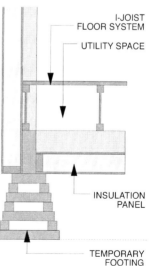

- ONE PLY ROOF SYSTEM
- INSULATION PANEL
- HOOK&BUILD FRAME
- I-JOIST FLOOR SYSTEM
- UTILITY SPACE
- INSULATION PANEL
- TEMPORARY FOOTING

cut-out pages of a study

EMERGENCY CONCEPTS

DESIGN CONCEPT FOR TSUNAMI DISASTER

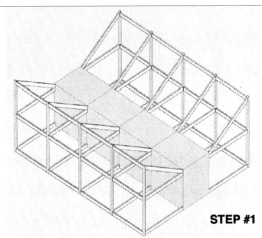

STEP #1

Connecting the HOOK&BUILD building system to the 40 feet metal container which was used to ship the system.

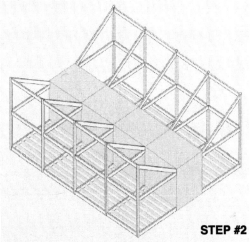

STEP #2

A floor joist system is installed in the new space.

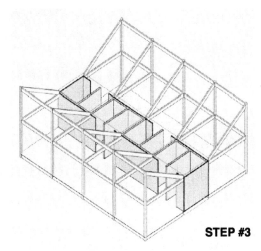

STEP #3

Dividing partitions are created to isolate the four living quarters from each other. All kitchens and bathrooms are in the container.

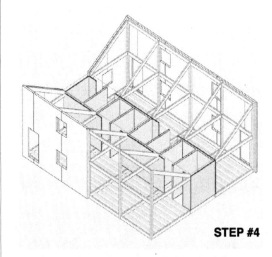

STEP #4

Insulated wall panels are erected around the living quarters. Four units are build per container. All plumbing is preinstalled in the floor and ceiling space of the container.

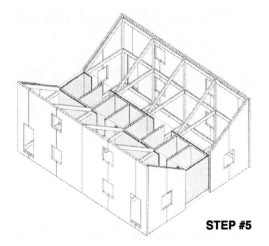

STEP #5

All insulated wall panels are in place, and finishing work can be done to the inside and outside when the roof panels and the roofing material is installed.

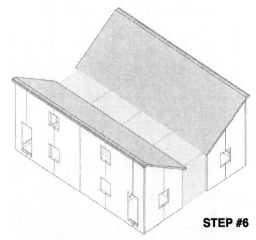

STEP #6

Roofing is finished, rainwater in the Monsun periods are guided towards the container, and collected in tanks or guided through channels to reservations.

RESOURCES

APA - The Engineered Wood Association
Tel: (253) 565-6600 Fax: (253) 565-7265
email: help@apawood.org
http://www.apawood.org

The Canadian Wood Council
Ottawa, Ontario, Canada, K1P 6B9
1-800-463-5091 Fax: (613) 747-6264
http://www.cwc.ca

Forintek Canada Corp. -
Tel: (604) 224-3221 Fax: (604) 222-5690
http://www.forintek.ca

Canadian Institute of Treated Wood (CITW)
Tel: (613) 737-4337
http://www.citw.org

Canadian Lumbermen's Association (CLA)
Tel: (613) 233-6205
http://www.cla-ca.ca

Canadian Plywood Association (CANPLY)
Tel: (604) 981-4190
http://www.canply.org

Canadian Wood Truss Association (CWTA)
Tel: (403) 271-0520
http://www.cwta.net

Coast Forest & Lumber Association (CFLA)
Tel: (604) 891-1237
http://www.cfla.org

Council of Forest Industries (COFI)
Tel: (604) 684-0211
http://www.cofi.org

Structural Board Association (SBA)
Tel: (905) 475-1100
http://www.osbguide.com

Straw Bale Construction Expert: Sustainable Works
Habib John Gonzalez
Te.: (250) 359-5095
E-mail: habibg@netidea.com
http://www.sustainableworks.ca

Structural Insulated Panel Association (SIP)
Tel: (253) 858-7472
www.sips.org

EPS Molders Association (SIPA)
Tel: (410) 451-8341 Fax: (410) 451-8343
http://www.epsmolders.org

British Urethane Foam Contractors Association (BUFCA)
Tel: (01428) 654011 Fax: (01428) 651401
http://www.bufca.co.uk/

Arxx Building Products
Toll free: 1-800-293-3210
Tel: 905-373-0004
Fax: 905-373-830
email: info@arxxwalls.com
http://www.arxxbuild.com

WORLD INDUSTRIES, INC.
Tel: (202) 624-3198 Fax: (202) 318-5373
http://www.isorast2000.com
Email: Isorast@worldindustries.biz

Plasti-Fab Edmonton
Tel: (780) 453-3718 Fax: (780) 452-0161
http://www.plastifab.com/main.html

Paragon Building Systems Inc.
Tel: (780)955-1067 Fax: (780)955-3710
http://www.paragonbuilding.ab.ca/
Email: sales@paragonbuilding.ab.ca

Advanced Panel Products Ltd.
Tel: (780) 955-6363 Fax: (780) 955-6377
Toll Free: 1-877-955-6363
E-mail: sales@advancedpanel.com
http://www.advancedpanel.com

ISBN 1425113311-1